Such a Dark Thing

Such a Dark Thing

Theology of the Vampire Narrative
in Popular Culture

M. Jess Peacock

RESOURCE *Publications* · Eugene, Oregon

SUCH A DARK THING
Theology of the Vampire Narrative in Popular Culture

Resource Publications
An Imprint of Wipf and Stock Publishers
199 W. 8th Ave., Suite 3
Eugene, OR 97401

www.wipfandstock.com

ISBN 13: 978-1-62032-719-7

Manufactured in the U.S.A.   02/03/2015

Dedicated to Allison, Michael and Julianne

I would totally turn you into vampires.

The basis of all true cosmic horror is violation of the order of nature, and the profoundest violations are always the least concrete and describable.

—H.P. LOVECRAFT, *SELECTED LETTERS III: 1929–1931*

To make you a vampire they have to suck your blood. And then you have to suck their blood. It's like a whole big sucking thing.

—BUFFY SUMMERS, *BUFFY THE VAMPIRE SLAYER*

Bring a vampire around, people start discovering religion.

—RICHARD LAYMON, *THE STAKE*

Contents

It's in the Blood

*"One thing about living in Santa Carla I never could stomach . . .
all the damn vampires."*

—*GRANDPA (BARNARD HUGHES) FROM* THE LOST BOYS[1]

IN 1979 I WAS eight years old, held aspirations of a career as a Jedi Knight,
and lived, as every eight year old should, oblivious to the fact that childhood
was a limited arrangement. It was on my eighth birthday, as a matter of fact,
when I settled in with my family to watch the highly anticipated CBS mini-
series *'Salem's Lot*.[2] Little did I know the effect that the movie would have on
my life, dropping me down a swirling rabbit hole of lifelong nerdom.[3]

It wasn't as if I were treading on some sort of virgin ground of horrific
gods and monsters. I watched Marty Sullivan's *Superhost* every Saturday
on WUAB 43, the local Cleveland television station where I received my
dose of Godzilla flicks, regular replays of the terribly underrated television
movie *Gargoyles* (1972),[4] Hammer horror films, and the expected parade
of Universal monsters (Dracula, Frankenstein, et al.). I was a well-seasoned

1. *The Lost Boys*, Schumacher, 1987.

2. The 1979 mini-series *'Salem's Lot* was originally slated to serve as the launching
pad for an ongoing television series starring David Soul.

3. From the Urban Dictionary: 1. The quality or state of being a nerd. 2. Of, or relating to, nerdiness.

4. Featuring circa 1972 creature effects from legendary special effects wizard Stan
Winston.

veteran of the creature feature thanks in large part to the waning days of Forrest J. Ackerman's publication *Famous Monsters of Filmland,*[5] as well as being the beneficiary of parents who saw nothing wrong with taking their kids to movies such as *Jaws 2* (1978) and *The Amityville Horror* (1979).

'Salem's Lot seemed to me be a different beast entirely. The commercials alone were terrifying, the story was based on a bestselling novel by Stephen King,[6] and television wasn't anywhere near the horror genre playground then that it is today. This was an entertainment event, one my parents were gracious enough to let me participate in, even knowing that I would end up irretrievably spooked and sleeping in their bed for the foreseeable future.

Despite this, I persevered through both nights of the frightening mini-series, my world irrevocably changed. How intensely my heart pounded when young Ralphie Glick emerged from the dense fog outside of his brother's window; the deathly scrape of dirty fingernails on glass, those dead yet piercing *eyes*, that malevolently hungry *smile*.[7] The visceral clutch of terror that gripped me when newly turned vampire Danny visited a sleeping Mark Petrie, commanding him, with equal parts conspiratorial whisper and animalistic hiss, to open the window. The living nightmare I suffered through when Mike Ryerson returned for school teacher Jason Burke, patiently sitting on a rocking chair in the guest room of the old man's home. These pale visages haunted my dreamscapes for countless nights, hovering above my bed as I slept, ravenous smiles leering at me from the impenetrable blackness of my closet, the door of which always seemed to be slightly ajar no matter how many times I closed it.

5. *Famous Monsters* boasts a stunning legacy of influence, with a Who's Who of genre staples attesting to their careers and imagination being stimulated by Ackerman and his publication. Legendary figures such as filmmaker Peter Jackson, special effects maestro Rick Baker, and even musician/filmmaker Rob Zombie have acknowledged their debt to *FM*. Zombie, in an interview I conducted with him in 2010, reminisced about the magazine, stating, "*Famous Monsters* was a part of that weird time period I remember as a kid during the late sixties monster boom. But there wasn't that much to be had for a typical kid. It seems absurd now because everything is everywhere, but I remember convincing our parents to drive us somewhere so we could buy *Famous Monsters* because that's all there was. And looking through them and thinking wow, check out all these movies that we'll never see! *Famous Monsters* of that time felt like a cool club. It wasn't judgmental, because everyone reading it loved monsters."

6. King had quickly become a literary phenomenon by this time with his novels *Carrie* and *The Shining,* the two novels that bookended 'Salem's Lot.

7. This particular moment from 'Salem's Lot was ranked by *Empire Magazine* as the fourth scariest movie scene of all time.

One might assume that exposure to the ghastly netherworld of horror at such a young age would have driven me to the lighter side of childish pursuits. Nevertheless, I found myself inexplicably drawn to the unsettling fear I experienced as I gazed out the window of my bedroom at night, wondering, in all of that darkness, if some malignant *thing* was staring right back at me.

After surviving the mini-series, I petitioned, pleaded with, and cajoled my parents into purchasing for me the novel *'Salem's Lot*. While only eight years old at the time, I was already a voracious reader, tearing through endless *Hardy Boys* novels, comic books, and whatever else passed for young adult literature during the waning years of the 1970s. My parents soon relented, and on a cold Christmas Eve in 1979, as my family traversed central Ohio visiting various relatives with a car full of wrapped presents, I commenced reading what would undoubtedly become my favorite novel of all time[8] and, in my estimation, one of the most important American novels of the twentieth century.

This is an important preface to the rest of *Such a Dark Thing: Theology of the Vampire Narrative in Popular Culture*. While I am an academic,[9] I am first and foremost a dyed in the wool, card carrying, was-watching-*Doctor Who*-in-the-seventies-before-it-was-trendy, nerd. Before hipsters paraded around in socially acceptable zombie walks, I poured over issues of *Fangoria*,[10] *Gorezone*, and *Starlog* in high school study hall, devoured the films of George Romero (*Dawn of the Dead*), Sam Raimi (*Evil Dead*[11]), and Don Coscarelli (*Phantasm*), and was purchasing prosthetics and finger extensions through mail order catalogs so I could transform myself into Count Orlok (Max Schreck) from the 1922 silent film masterpiece *Nosferatu*. My childhood and adolescence were, for better or for worse, reflective of the boys in the film *The Monster Squad* (1987), a movie that served as a manifesto of everything I loved about life and pop culture. Oh, and did I mention I was somewhat of a social pariah as a result?

---

8. The cover of my paperback of *'Salem's Lot*, which was purchased from a local used bookstore, was frightening to behold; a solid black cover featuring an embossed black mask of a little girl, a single drop of red blood dangling from the corner of her lips.

9. Translation: A geek with a large vocabulary.

10. On several occasions my mom was the recipient of phone calls from various teachers concerned with the gore and horror they would glimpse over my shoulder as I read *Fangoria* in study hall.

11. I have the autograph of Bruce Campbell, the star of the *Evil Dead* trilogy of movies, tattooed on my left arm.

I am a fanboy.[12] I love horror and take the genre seriously, as evidenced by the zombie tattoos covering my arm and the Library of Congress catalog number for the novel 'Salem's Lot on my lower leg. And I eventually discovered that my academic interests in religion, mythology, and social justice movements dovetailed nicely with a brand of storytelling that, at its best, not only touched on all three, it also boasted frightening and spectacular monsters. From the social commentary of George Romero's zombie films, to the unintentional Judeo-Christian morality play of the Friday the 13th franchise,[13] to the plethora of science versus God themes perfectly embodied in James Whale's Frankenstein (1931)[14] and its endless progeny such as the excellent 2009 film Splice, the horror genre is rife with narrative complexity.

I took this arguably overzealous love of horror into my early career as a student pastor. I regularly introduced clips from genre movies, encouraging students to view film and the horror genre as an allegorical tool. More often than not I had to explain to angry parents why I was showing movie clips of Christopher Lee's Dracula being defeated with two candleholders in the shape of a cross wielded by Peter Cushing's Van Helsing.[15]

So, dear reader, I make this pledge to you: I will do my best to avoid the dry, joyless academic blather that can often accompany a book of this nature.[16] Sure, there is the requisite technical mumbo jumbo that goes

---

12. From the Urban Dictionary: A passionate fan of various elements of geek culture (e.g. sci-fi, comics, Star Wars, video games, anime, hobbits, Magic: the Gathering, etc.), but who lets his passion override social graces.

13. Don't drink, don't smoke, don't do drugs, and abstain from having sex, lest ye be judged by Jason Voorhees (or his mother, if we're being technical). Sounds positively Old Testament.

14. In the original version of the 1931 film Frankenstein, Colin Clive's Dr. Frankenstein, upon successfully animating his monstrous creation, proclaims, "Now I know what it feels like to be God!"

15. "It's about sin . . . and redemption . . . and . . . and . . . oh never mind."

16. Kim Paffenroth, a professor of religious studies and author of several works of zombie fiction including the Dying to Live series, penned one of the more interesting scholarly deconstructions of a horror sub-genre with his book Gospel of the Living Dead: George Romero's Visions of Hell on Earth (Baylor University Press, 2006), an exhaustive look at the sociological and theological implications of the undead cinematic portfolio of George Romero. And even though I am analyzing and discussing the vampire sub-genre with regard to Christian theology, I felt that Paffenroth's focus on Romero's zombie milieu might be worth a quick examination here at the outset, both in tone and process, as it served as the operating ethos for Such a Dark Thing.

Paffenroth examines the various issues at play in Romero's zombie films (both symbolic and overt) such as sin and redemption, consumerism and materialism, racism,

along with any research project. However, my hope is that you will have fun reading *Such a Dark Thing*. After all, we're discussing vampires! And if a discussion of vampires should be anything, it should be *fun*, not an annoying and horrendously dull slog of pretentious self-involvement.[17]

---

sexism, and class warfare to name only a few. For example, with regard to *Land of the Dead*, the author writes, "It is not the military, government, or church that exercises real power, but the wealthy . . . according to Romero, the White House, the Pentagon, and the Vatican do not run or exploit the world — Wall Street does" (125). This type of critical analysis of what some might write off as a mindlessly violent film gives *Gospel of the Living Dead* a resonance that a general analysis of the Romero library might not provide.

Paffenroth particularly excels when dissecting the theology of the undead, a task made difficult in light of the overt anti-religion stance George Romero has assumed over the years, both cinematically and personally. "More than any other movie monster or mythological creature," Paffenroth writes, "Zombies vividly show the state of damnation, of human life without the Divine gift of reason, and without any hope of change or improvement" (23). It is from this unique perspective that the author analyzes potential theological springboards in the films, avoiding, for the most part, heavy-handed allegorical images.

Gospel of the Living Dead provides an important analysis of a body of work that has always had more on its mind than bloodlust and gut munching. Paffenroth takes George Romero, the horror genre, and fans of the zombie sub-genre seriously, and dives headlong into not only an apologetic of Romero's seminal work, but a true celebration of the social and theological layers buried within.

17. I'm looking at you *Twilight*.

Acknowledgments

As EVIDENCED IN THE preface, the roots of my horror obsession originate with my parents, particularly my father. I have very fond memories of our excursions to the three-screen movie theater in Ashland, Ohio in order to survey the latest horror fare. *Silent Rage* (1982), *Friday the 13th III: 3D* (1982), *Fright Night* (1985), *Aliens* (1986), *Christine* (1983), *One Dark Night* (1982), *Creepshow* (1982), *Poltergeist* (1982), and *A Nightmare on Elm Street* (1984) are just a few of the fright flicks we braved together, not to mention the countless schlock classics we discovered during the VHS revolution. He died far too young at fifty years of age, and I like to think we'd still be catching the occasional horror film together.

In addition, my mom deserves a considerable amount of credit for not censoring my taste for the horror genre and actually defending her son from authority figures that tried to quell his interests. In today's environment, a student who suddenly cut his hair into a mullet and started wearing a long black coat in order to emulate Keifer Sutherland from *The Lost Boys*, while being about thirty years behind the times, might be a source of consternation for his parents. My mom, however, saw a creative and imaginative mind, and for that I will always be grateful.

Sarah Knapke Arevalo, while a strong supporter during the last couple months of completing the manuscript, deserves a specific thank you for her input and fact checking on the *Twilight* book series. Thanks, Sarah, I really, really didn't want to do it.

When I decided that I wanted to enter graduate school in my late thirties and study, of all things, religion, my wife of barely one year didn't even flinch, and ultimately gave far too much of herself to support us while I toiled away researching, writing, and occasionally leaving town to present papers at various academic conferences. It was during those years that *Such a Dark Thing* took shape, and my efforts and contacts in grad school directly led to its publication. Allison has been an endless source of love, encouragement, and motivation while I wrote this book. She also lets me hang my *'Salem's Lot* posters in the living room, which makes her a keeper.

Speaking of contacts, Dr. Tim Van Meter, an associate professor at Methodist Theological School in Ohio (MTSO), who supervised a modest independent study I developed on the theology of the vampire narrative, strongly urged me to submit the finalized project as a book proposal to Wipf & Stock where he was also writing a manuscript at the time. That seemed to work out ok for me.

It's a shame that the publisher won't let me name this book *Would Not Exist Without Yvonne Zimmerman*, because, well, it's true. Dr. Zimmerman, also an associate professor at MTSO, was an enormous influence on this project and on me as an academician. Her encouragement, guidance, pep talks, and friendship kept me motivated not only throughout the ups and downs of grad school, she also helped to keep my eyes on the prize of completing the manuscript when I saw it more as a burden and less as a privilege. Yeah, she's getting a free copy.

There were several factors that coalesced to inspire this book, one of the most influential being my time at MTSO. It was there that I learned to view the exploration and dissection of Christian theology similar to that of a detective working toward the resolution of a crime: let the facts lead you to the truth. And while cold hard data in theological studies is somewhat equivalent to the existence of a magical unicorn, we as academics must cut through centuries of creeds and dogma to ultimately discover what the act of unquestioned belief in an omnipotent and omniscient deity, one that narratively allows (and in some cases instigates) immense suffering within the world, really means for the larger faith community. Religion, Christianity in particular, is not, nor has it ever been, immutable, despite what many might think. My time at MTSO taught me that, throughout history, religion has adapted to the larger culture, and as such an ideological and narrative reformation is needed now more than ever. Contemporary religion must evolve beyond the antiquated laws, doctrine, and theologies that prevent modern audiences from fully embracing it and develop into a vibrant mosaic of transcendent and transforming narratives, which is ultimately the overriding message of *Such a Dark Thing*.

There are many other individuals who should be thanked here for their support and encouragement. My concern would be forgetting someone and hurting feelings, so let me convey my appreciation to everyone who took an interest (or at least feigned curiosity) in my nerdy little project. Every kind word of encouragement was needed and valued.

Religious Shadows: The Vampire as Divine Narrative

"Somebody once asked me if I have anything like faith, and I said I have faith in the narrative. I have a belief in a narrative that is bigger than me, that is alive and I trust will work itself out."

—*JOSS WHEDON*[1]

IN THE 1985 FILM *Fright Night,* teenager Charley Brewster (William Ragsdale) discovers that an ancient vampire has moved into the house next door to him. Obviously in over his head and fearful for his life after the vampire, Jerry Dandridge (Chris Sarandon), attacks him in his own home,[2] Charley desperately approaches Peter Vincent[3] (Roddy McDowall), an aged host of a late night cable access horror show, for assistance in dispatching the fiend. Vincent, misunderstanding the intent of Charley and believing he desires an autograph, informs the boy that his show has just been cancelled. "[N]obody wants to see vampire killers anymore, or vampires either.

1. "Joss Whedon: The Definitive EW Interview," *Entertainment Weekly,* September 1, 2014.

2. Charley's mom invites Dandridge into the house earlier that evening in an attempt to gauge his romantic availability. "With my luck, he's probably gay."

3. The name Peter Vincent is an amalgamation paying tribute to Peter Cushing and Vincent Price, two legendary actors within the horror genre. Price was originally pursued for the role but declined.

Apparently all they want to see are demented madmen running around in ski-masks, hacking up young virgins."[4]

This condemnation of the post-modern horror genre, particularly with regard to the neglect of the vampire sub-genre in the mid-1980s,[5] has proven to be paradoxically prophetic and myopic. While the television series *Buffy the Vampire Slayer* arguably primed contemporary culture in the relatively fangless 1990s for an imminent vampiric invasion of popular entertainment, it was the nascent days of the twenty-first century where the mythological beast truly exploded in popularity, from the cultural phenomena of the *Twilight* young adult book and film series,[6] to *True Blood* and *The Vampire Diaries* on television, to any number of video games, best selling novels, and innumerable websites devoted to the undead.

The physical representation of the vampire is traditionally human in nature, making it familiar and relatable, the mythic lore malleable enough to adapt to a wide range of rapidly changing cultural, societal, and entertainment needs, evidenced by the survival of the undead in the western consciousness since Bram Stoker put ink to paper.[7] Academician Susannah Clements expands on this notion in her book *The Vampire Defanged: How the Embodiment of Evil Became a Romantic Hero* when she writes, "We can make a vampire mean what we want it to mean. We can use it for any number of purposes . . . there is something about the figure of the vampire that attracts us in this metaphorical sense. As a metaphor it hits at the heart of what makes us human."[8]

The vampire throughout history has represented everything from the LGBTQI community, forbidden love, seductive and corrupting forces

---

4. *Fright Night*, Holland, 1985.

5. While there are a few notable exceptions (e.g. *The Lost Boys, Near Dark*), horror of the 1980s was memorably dominated by mass murderers such as Jason and Freddy.

6. Arguments and countless Internet memes abound as to whether Edward from the *Twilight* series and his ilk should even be considered vampires at all. A personal favorite representation of this view can be found on a t-shirt from Fright-Rags.com where David, Keifer Sutherland's teenage vampire from the film *The Lost Boys*, is brandishing a large knife in one hand and the severed head of Robert Pattinson's Edward from the film version of *Twilight* clutched in the other hand. Carved into Edward's head are the words, "I Ruined Vampires."

7. It should be noted that the "penny dreadful" *Varney the Vampire or the Feast of Blood* by James Malcolm Rymer preceded the novel *Dracula* by roughly fifty years (and indeed heavily influenced it in many respects). However, Stoker's vision of the undead cemented for all time the mythology within the cultural imagination.

8. Clements, *The Vampire Defanged*, 4.

threatening the institution of marriage, the political and social *other,* immigrants endangering the very fabric of civilized society, and the interpersonal dynamics of the family. Even the seemingly mindless vampire hordes represented in movies such as the exceptional *Stake Land*[9] (2011) and the graphic novel inspired film *30 Days of Night* (2007) provide a tapestry for talented artists to explore endless topics and allegories under the microscope of the tragedy and trauma brought about as a result of the external weight of the vampire. Scott Poole writes of monsters serving as "'meaning machines' . . . excavating all manner of cultural productions depending on their context and their historical moment."[10] Whether intentioned or not, the vampire cannot help but be saddled with the allegorical baggage that a particular culture requires.

That said, the vampire is most commonly viewed as a symbol of sin, temptation, Satan, and even God. This is sometimes addressed directly, such as in Bram Stoker's novel *Dracula* or the films *Dracula 2000* (2000) and the aforementioned *Fright Night,* and often indirectly, such as in the television series *Buffy the Vampire Slayer,* the movie *Blade* (1998), or *The Strain* series of novels. Standing mute without additional commentary, the figure of the vampire is, from a western perspective, undeniably religious as it, knowingly or not, seeks to make a statement on the natural human fear of death, the promise of resurrection, and the hope for everlasting life.

Any analysis of the vampire in popular culture that does not take into account the deep religious roots of the creature is a shortsighted and incomplete one, as the vampire inarguably exudes a spiritual aura simply through its imaginative existence. In his novel *Dracula,* Bram Stoker's literary allusion to the Christian exercise of Holy Communion, represented in Mina Harker being forced to drink the blood of Dracula, is only one suggestion of the religious nature of the vampire. As we shall examine, Dracula granting eternal life through an unholy Eucharist reflects a not too subtle religious sensibility, rocketing the vampire into the controversial and arguable status of Christ figure.

Whether used as a direct illustration or nothing more than a whisper of a metaphor, the vampire narrative deals with issues of the soul, the hope for a life hereafter, and the potential of forces beyond our control to deface or even destroy that hope. The default conversation surrounding the soul in

---

9. *Stake Land,* while a fantastic piece of low budget filmmaking, felt more like an exercise in zombie apocalypse fare. But, technically, it *was* a vampire film.

10. Poole, *Monsters in America,* xiv.

vampire narratives is the most important clue as to the religious nature of the vampire and the mythos surrounding it. Douglas Cowan, in his excellent analysis of horror films entitled *Sacred Terror: Religion and Horror on the Silver Screen*, writes, "All but ubiquitous in horror cinema, whether tormented, at rest, or the object of supernatural conflict, the soul is an explicitly religious concept, one that makes little sense apart from the various religious frameworks in which it comes embedded."[11] In other words, the very presence of the vampire in a narrative, a creature that has refused death, either choosing or condemned to an existence trapped between the worlds of the living and the dead, whether overtly religious in the mold of Count Dracula, or seemingly entirely secular as modeled by Marlow[12] from the *30 Days of Night* universe, speaks to a theological or religious nature. And while artists, writers, and filmmakers will likely never grow weary of squeezing new narratives, meanings, and cultural markers from this tirelessly innovative and adaptable figure, it is quite nearly impossible to not acknowledge the religious nucleotides that comprise the western vampire mythos.

Religion and vampires find themselves enmeshed in an intimate, if not entirely comfortable, embrace, where even the most spiritually abstinent individual can identify the symbolic arsenal and demonic presence the vampire carries through the valley of popular culture. Cowan adds "the demonic is a dyadic concept; it only really makes religious sense in terms of the Divine. Thus, it is not unimportant that these narrative crises are predicated on a religiously oriented universe."[13] The vampire, while immortal, presents a myriad of very human questions and fears around issues of life and death. Why does the vampire reject death, preferring the ineffable twilight realm, neither living nor dead, to a destination of eternal finality? Whether a refusal to commune *with* or *before* the Divine, or even an inability to accept spiritual oblivion, the presence of the vampire is to hold company with theological and spiritual uncertainty. That uncertainty, screaming throughout the fictional universe of the undead, is nightmarish in its implications, a prehistoric anxiety over the fear that the next world is not what we hope it to be. As Mary Hallab writes in *Vampire God: The Allure of the Undead in Western Culture*, "Even when no reference is made to religion or the afterlife,

---

11. Cowan, *Sacred Terror,* 6.

12. Steve Niles, creator of the *30 Days of Night* comic book series, has openly acknowledged that the name of Marlow is a tip of the hat to Barlow, the master vampire from Stephen King's *Salem's Lot.*

13. Cowan, *Sacred Terror,* 90.

the vampire teases us with dreams of transcendence and of defeating death on this earth."[14] The vampire stands as a mythical portent, a transcendent figure warning us that all may not be as we hope and believe, and that the horror of the afterlife is worth rebelling against.

Despite this, while the vampire narrative has exploded in esteem within the cultural zeitgeist over the last decade, the overt religious underpinnings that have made it such a fascinating theological figure have waned, with exceptions such as the film *Dracula 2000*, which painted the legendary vampire as a vengeful Judas Iscariot, only proving the rule. The aforementioned lament of Peter Vincent with regard to the horror genre gives voice to this shift within the vampire narrative, which itself may be a post-modern testament to the diminishing influence of religion within contemporary culture overall.[15] Clements writes, "As the vampire myth was first turned into fiction, the associations of the vampire with evil and temptation were established, characteristics that have been diminishing gradually since."[16] She continues with, "As the figure of the vampire in contemporary culture becomes increasingly secular, the spiritual and theological potential in the vampire is gradually being lost."[17] While later in this book I will take issue with certain aspects of the analysis made by Clements regarding the western vampire myth in popular culture, she is absolutely correct in pointing out that the characteristics of the modern vampire, despite serving as a theological figure simply through its fantastical existence, has become far less religiously overt over the last thirty years.

Modern cultural considerations aside, the vampire throughout history still stands as a potent theological totem, rife with symbolism, metaphorical power, and, perhaps, the religious admonition of what happens when one fails to abide by the precepts of God. By being presented as the inversion of the Divine, the vampire comes to embody all that one must avoid should they hope for right standing within their particular faith and eternal peace after they pass into the next world. From a narrative standpoint, this dualism brings meaning and order to the inherently chaotic nature of life, presenting a simple choice between good (the will of God embodied in the

14. Hallab, *Vampire God,* 128.

15. Granted, this statement is a bit abstract and difficult to prove. However, many studies reflect the steady decline in church attendance in mainline denominations.

16. Clements, *Vampire Defanged,* 4.

17. Ibid., 162.

various sacred icons and applied machineries of deliverance[18]) and evil (the will of the vampire embodied in lust, power, inverted religious practices, and eternal life devoid of spiritual fulfillment). Timothy Beal, in his book *Religion and Its Monsters,* argues, "The politically and religiously conservative function of the monstrous is to encourage one to pull back from the edge . . . They literally scare the hell out of us."[19]

The vampire, however, serves as more than a fundamentalist boogeyman shambling through the conservative religious imagination of moral gatekeepers. It provides the unique opportunity for those so inclined to bestow flesh and vivacity to theological concepts hiding in the darker realms of religious studies (e.g. theodicy, ritual blood sacrifice, etc.) The very existence of the vampire, that of a human conquering death, whether as a result of a curse, sheer willpower, or some other fictional contrivance,[20] is a thumb in the eye to the dogmatic propaganda surrounding the role of God as the unquestioned magnate of life and death. While the religiously shallow and uneducated piously resort to bumper sticker doctrine, standing in righteous judgment of anyone who travels down these darkened theological corridors, the vampire narrative within popular culture offers an incomparable window into not only theological uncertainties, it propositions, as we will discuss in the final chapter of this book, a message of resistance and of liberation from oppression.

The existence of the vampire enables us to grapple with and examine these potentially dangerous empires of deliberation. Even so, some might still bristle at the notion of an undead creature that rises from the grave in order to drink the blood of unsuspecting victims operating as a theological marker. It should be noted, however, that monsters, the horrific, and religion are more enmeshed than some might suspect, or perhaps be comfortable with admitting. Poole, in his book *Monsters in America,*[21] writes of the association between the religious and the monstrous:

---

18. These machineries include the cross, holy water, the wafer, sacred space, confession etc.

19. Beal, *Religion and Its Monsters,* 195.

20. In the film *Byzantium* (2012), the vampiric conversion process involves entering a cave where one interestingly meets (and is killed by) their doppelganger.

21. Nobody could be blamed for mistaking *Monsters In America* for a book that it simply is not. Whether a result of the title itself, or the gnarled trees shrouded in an ominous fog serving as the cover art, this is not some compendium of hauntings in the heartland or a documentation of personal eyewitnesses to the antics of the Jersey Devil. Author and history professor W. Scott Poole has constructed a work that is far more

The Latin word *monstrum* provides us with our English term *mon-ster*. *Monstrum* is "that which appears" or reveals itself ... Monsters have been, from ancient times, invested with meanings Divine and demonic, theological or fearfully natural. In every society they appear as multifaceted beings composed of a complicated tangle of symbolic synapses, living messages to those unlucky souls to whom they appear.[22]

Whether it be Leviathan and Behemoth in the Hebrew Bible, Satan and his army of fallen angels, or the menagerie of uncanny monsters at the conclusion of the New Testament,[23] religion, particularly Christianity, knows and is familiar with the monstrous. One could even make a legitimate argument that God represents the most diabolical, violent, and blood-thirsty monster of all, an otherworldly ancient deity that takes no issue with the detached murder of countless innocent lives in order to punish those deemed as irretrievably wicked. The narrative of the flood and the plagues of Egypt paint a disturbingly dark picture of a supposedly loving deity, a reminder of the wrinkles and coarseness we discover when stepping into the theological shadows.

in-depth, scholarly, and imaginative than any throw-away bargain bin schlock that fills the bookshelves every autumn, and has set the bar ridiculously high for any future re-search exploring the locus of historical and cultural studies, particularly as it pertains to the horrific.

Equal parts thoughtful and frightening, *Monsters In America* explores the darkest recesses of American history, using the distorted reflection of fictional monstrosities to tease out the true horror of this nation's unflattering past, ideologies, and political and religious nightmares uniquely suited to these shores.

Monsters In America is not a simple Sunday stroll through analogous genre icons as they pertain to interesting footnotes in American history. Poole has written an important text that serves as a clarion call for readers to closely examine the commonly accepted narrative of history that has been steadily spoon fed to a people who want to, *need* to, believe in the overt goodness of America. Monsters, Poole successfully argues, serve to pull back the membranous protective tissue of historical revisionism to reveal the char-nel house of injustice and lies found beneath.

From Mary Shelley's *Frankenstein* serving as a metaphor of slave rebellion, to the monstrous Saturday matinee mutations standing in for the horrors of The Love Canal tragedy, to a resurgence in the popularity of the *Universal* Monsters in the 1970's serving as an anchor for kids living through the restructuring of the American family, *Monsters In America* challenges, enlightens, and, quite honestly, shocks in its prescient view of American history, as well as the seeming ubiquity of the monsters of our past and prob-able future.

22. Poole, *Monsters in America*, 5.

23. Dracula actually means *dragon*, linking Bram Stoker's character even more so with Christian sensibility (that of eschatological imagery), even if it is as an anti-Christ.

In addition to these anxieties, what does the supposedly benevolent act of Holy Communion have to say about the unspoken, dark, and more horrific elements of contemporary Christianity? Namely, what the purpose and meaning of communion might be able to teach us about the nature of God, and whether that nature is truly worthy of adoration and devotion. The vampire narrative within popular culture ultimately functions as our portal into this disturbing world of theological insecurity, and builds the creative space by which we can explore the furthest regions of the sacred and the profane. To borrow a line from the demon Pinhead of *Hellraiser* fame, the vampire has such sights to show us.

It's Symbolism That's Important, Never Truth: The Monstrous Divine I

The Joss Whedon and Drew Goddard co-written film *The Cabin in the Woods* (2012) has been widely praised by critics across the ideological and entertainment spectrum for many reasons. From its deconstruction of traditional horror tropes, to its critique of our contemporary surveillance society, to a scathing rebuke of the cultural obsession with youth and ultimately destroying said youth, to the timely metaphor of mundane individuals in pristine office buildings controlling and manipulating the horrors of contemporary society, *The Cabin in the Woods* is a movie that is deeply layered and nuanced, while simultaneously broad enough to cover a large swath of symbolic and metaphorical ground.

Seemingly nothing more than a tired retread of familiar horror acreage, Whedon and Goddard have succeeded at crafting a sociological and theological weathervane for the twenty-first century and, while not a vampire film (although there is a brief appearance by a vampire), is being briefly used here to initiate a longer conversation we will be conducting on religious themes that the vampire can often be seen to represent.

Within the film, four college-aged students find themselves the unwitting victims of a mysterious ritual designed to appease slumbering giant evil gods, powerful Lovecraftian ancient ones that would, should the ritual fail, awaken and destroy the planet. Apparently run by a top-secret government organization, the elaborate sacred ceremony involves the violent death of the victims (required by the gods to be a jock, a stoner, a whore, a scholar, and a virgin) at the hands of the terrifying horror genre trope they unwittingly choose (e.g. zombies, killer clowns, mermen, etc.)

Prior to the start of the ritual, after technicians from various departments of the shadowy organization have placed bets on whichever indescribable terror would be raised by the unsuspecting youth, two staff members, newbie Truman (Brian White) and the jaded Lin (Amy Acker), engage in the following exchange:

TRUMAN: Monsters, magic, gods . . .

LIN: You get used to it.

TRUMAN: Should you?[24]

For Truman, the violent religious ritual is a visceral, raw, and unspeakable scenario. For Lin, however, familiarity has bred indifference. The scope of her actions and the small part she is playing in a larger cosmic narrative has been dimmed by the mendacity of her duty as a cog in the wheel of this dark method to appease the slumbering gods. In some regard, the same thing has happened to contemporary Christians who stumble through their various scriptures, dogmas, and rituals that, it would seem, serve to appease the desires and wrath of a mysterious and potentially horrific God.

Make no mistake, western religion and the vampire narrative within popular culture are closely enmeshed dueling discourses on the unknown, of what lies beyond human reason and understanding, an issue at the forefront of *The Cabin in the Woods*. Whedon and Goddard highlight how the requirement of a blood sacrifice by a deity reveals unquestioned (at least for religious practitioners) horrors. As a result of this Jungian suppression of the dark side of the Divine, the horror genre has emerged as the silhouette of religion, quite literally it would seem in the world of *The Cabin in the Woods* where, it is important to note, the structure and process designed to keep the slumbering monsters at bay is a distinctly religious one. For example, after ritualistic whore Jules (Anna Hutchison) is brutally slaughtered at the hands of the demented Buckner family, *de facto* ceremonial priest Sitterson (Richard Jenkins) kisses a symbol attached to a necklace he is wearing and intones, "This we offer in humility and fear, for the blessed peace of your eternal slumber. As it ever was."[25]

For the unfortunate victims within the film, they soon find their lives shattered by a type of atonement sacrificial worship service run by an unseen cabal of puppeteers who inflict on the innocent youth enough

24. *The Cabin in the Woods*, Goddard, 2012.
25. Ibid., Goddard.

violence, suffering, and death to put them on par with the mythical figure of Job, who also never quite knew the source of his torment. In addition, while the character of Satan in the Job narrative conducted his business at the behest of an apathetic if not a slumbering God, Sitterson and Hadley appropriately fill a similar role for their cosmic overlords.

Through their pain and suffering, Marty the stoner (Fran Kanz) and Dana the virgin (Kristen Connolly) come to identify with the inversion of the natural order and the chaos that would be brought about if the slumbering gods were to awaken and walk the earth once more. In their conversation with the Director (Sigourney Weaver), it is made very clear to them that, should this ritual fail, the world would be irrevocably doomed. Marty replies, "Maybe that's the way it ought to be. Maybe it's time for a change." The Director, aghast, says, "We're not talking about change. We're talking about the agonizing death of every human soul on the planet."[26]

Later, as the two students lay bleeding, casually smoking a joint and waxing rhapsodic about the end of the world, Dana says, "Humanity . . . pfft. It's time to give someone else a chance."[27] Marty and Dana have set their faces against the created order and have aligned themselves, as a result of their pain and suffering, with chaos and darkness (a concept that will be discussed through the lens of the Job narrative at greater length).

It becomes difficult to discern who is truly a monster and who is a God within the world of *The Cabin in the Woods*. Are not Hadley and Sitterson in some manner representative of godlike figures? At their fingertips are the tools to control and manipulate others, and even to take their lives, or at least allow their lives to be taken. At the same time, this power is rather monstrous, their indifferent actions resulting in the death of innocent men and women (although their power is not absolute and they are subject to a force far more powerful and sinister than they could possibly account for). In addition, while Dana and Marty spend the movie fighting, unknowingly, against the power and influence of the slumbering gods, they come to identify with them in the end, allowing them to rise and destroy the earth and everyone on it. This decision is also at once godlike and monstrous, as they hold the fate of billions in their hands.

26. Ibid., Goddard.
27. Ibid., Goddard.

Drunk With Blood: The Monstrous Divine II

In his classic sermon "Sinners in the Hands of an Angry God," Jonathan Edwards describes a deity whose wrath "is like great waters that are dammed for the present; they increase more and more, and rise higher and higher, till an outlet is given, and the longer the stream is stopped, the more rapid and mighty is its course, when once it is let loose."[28] He continues to paint an ominous and menacing portrait of a type of blood god, similar to that of the demon Shezmu who served as the Egyptian god of slaughter, eternally waiting to unleash violence and destruction on wayward followers:

> The bow of God's wrath is bent, and the arrow made ready on the string, and justice bends the arrow at your heart, and strains the bow, and it is nothing but the mere pleasure of God, and that of an angry God, without any promise or obligation at all, that keeps the arrow one moment from being made drunk with your blood . . . you are thus in the hands of an angry God; 'tis nothing but his mere pleasure that keeps you from being this moment swallowed up in everlasting destruction.[29]

The God raging within the theology of Jonathan Edwards is filled with unbridled wrath for the inhabitants of the terrestrial world who are required to appease this monstrous otherworldly force, one poised to unleash its omnipotent fury at a moments notice, held back, in the Hebrew Bible, only through ritual sacrifices of animal blood. Eventually this God demanded the sacramental scapegoating of Jesus of Nazareth, perhaps the most legendary act of filicide found in popular mythology. Subsequently, Christians are generally expected to relive this sacrifice through the act of communion, whereby they symbolically (or literally, through the process of *transubstantiation*) drink the blood and eat the flesh of the demigod Jesus in order to appease the furious almighty deity passionately preached by Edwards, thereby preventing the full wrath of an angry God from being visited upon creation. Whether viewed literally or symbolically, this testifies to a troubling relationship between the Creator and the created that is rarely discussed within western mainline denominational settings.

As illustrated in the film *The Cabin in the Woods*, familiarity breeds indifference. A similar consequence has transpired with regard to Christianity and its various rituals that, it would seem, serve to appease the

---

28. Edwards, *A Jonathan Edwards Reader*, 96.
29. Ibid., 97.

desires and wrath of a mysterious deity. Put another way, if God is benevolent and worthy of worship and exaltation, then why the need for a
ritual sacrifice, symbolic as it might be? Is there really such a strong appetite for gods of wrath, violence, and mass genocide amongst modern
religious communities?

While contemporary Protestant theologies have attempted to smooth
over the rougher edges of some of the more horrific aspects of the Judeo-
Christian mythos, it is still difficult to ignore the intrinsic dreadfulness that
must occur when external and unknown powers intersect with terra firma.
For millions of believers around the world, a God is worshipped who established power and dominance through acts of unspeakable violence, blood-
shed, and destruction. The story of Noah conveys the capriciousness of
God resulting in the destruction of nearly all of humanity, and the action/
adventure eschatology of the *Left Behind* series of novels paints a picture of
a vengeful God returning to this planet drenched in the blood of all those
who refuse to kneel in worship. Giant evil gods indeed!

Depending on the theological perspective, the slumbering, nefarious gods and elaborate rituals associated with the horrific imagination of
author H.P. Lovecraft might bear a striking resemblance to what can be
seen and heard around the world every Sunday at many Christian worship services. Nathan D. Mitchell writes in *Meeting Mystery*, "Ritual leads to
revelation . . . God's Word never merely speaks; it also *does*, acts, confronts
worshipers with the troubling prospect of a revelation they may not wish
to hear or see[.]"[30] And while Mitchell was referring to revelations of grace
and guidance, this passage is equally perceptive with regard to the more
diabolical disclosures, traits, and aspects of the Divine that are revealed
through various religious rituals such as the ancient Christian communal
sacrifice of flesh and blood.

As noted, one only has to breeze through the Hebrew Bible to understand that the nature of Yahweh is not simply one of nobility and rightful-
ness. There is a palpable element of fear derived from the power of life and
death wielded by the Divine over the mortal plane, the mythological ability
to wipe humanity from the face of the earth on a whim. The Creator, seen
less as a nurturer and more as a mercurial cosmic overlord who demands,
above all else, faithfulness, is regularly portrayed within Scripture as also
inhabiting the role of a Destroyer. Beal writes, "There are indeed monsters
in the Bible, inspiring not a little horror. Indeed, one might say that the

30. Mitchell, *Meeting Mystery*, 133.

Bible is literally *riddled* with monsters . . . the relation between the biblical God and these monsters is particularly riddling and disturbing."[31] It is this often troubling relationship between gods and monsters, the sacred and the profane, and cosmogony and chaos, that shelters questions as to the role of the Divine in the enmeshment of good and evil and the disquieting understanding that "the diabolic is firmly embedded in Christian Scripture, mythistory, and worship."[32]

The vampire, then, rests among well-established religious company, emerging from the swirling darkness of the chaos lurking at the seems of creation not only to strike fear within the heart of eager audiences, it exists, perhaps unknowingly, as a lens through which to view death, questions of evil, the search for transcendent meaning, and where exactly God fits into it all. The image of the vampire in literary and cinematic history provides a unique opportunity to examine any number of theological issues as well as pressing societal concerns. Foremost among these avenues of inquiry is the relationship between the mortal and the Divine and how that transpires amongst a world of moral evil and very real monsters that leave genuine victims in their wake. And much like the vampire and other fictional demons of our day, the real terrors that we must address as a society are never quite dead and buried, eternally coming back for one more scare, one more kill, one more tragedy. From the resurgence of racially based voter suppression tactics supposedly staked soon after the Jim Crow era, to the ongoing religiously motivated assaults on women and the LGBTQI community, to a perpetual American culture of war, to the growing scourge of human sex and labor trafficking, to the influence of corporate money in the modern political process, to the increasing threat of poverty and homelessness, our fiends are real, they are both spiritual and physical in nature, and they are growing in destructive force.

What can the vampire bring to the table as we examine its place within the religious narrative and the theological implications of our everyday monsters? While discussions of theology are often only reserved for far more pious settings than the horror genre, and inquiries of a philosophical nature are generally relegated to the realm of academia, the vampire succeeds at intersecting these disciplines within contemporary culture in an accessible and relevant manner, effectively providing us a symbol through which both cosmic questions and perceptible real world issues can be addressed. As

31. Beal, *Religion and Its Monsters*, 25.
32. Cowan, *Sacred Terror*, 176.

Hallab concludes, "[T]he vampire leads us to a larger consideration of the nature of the individual and his search for significance in a vast and terrifying universe."[33] However, before we can fully discuss these larger considerations, we must first venture further into the imaginative crypt of the vampire, excavating what truly makes it such an intoxicating religious figure.

33. Hallab, *Vampire God*, 1.

1

OMG!: The Vampire as Mysterium Tremendum

*"How pathetic it is to describe these things
which can't truly be described."*[1]

—*LOUIS, FROM* INTERVIEW WITH
THE VAMPIRE *BY ANNE RICE*

AT THE CLIMAX OF the novel *'Salem's Lot* by Stephen King, Ben Mears, the author turned reluctant vampire killer, has finally come face-to-face with Barlow, his undead antagonist. As the sun sets and the showdown begins, the master vampire psychically invades the mind of Mears, declaring:

> Look and see me, puny man. Look upon Barlow, who has passed the centuries as you have passed hours before a fireplace with a book. Look and see the great creature of the night whom you would slay with your miserable little stick. Look upon me, scribbler. I have written in human lives, and blood has been my ink. Look upon me and despair![2]

Faced with the overwhelming power of his otherworldly adversary, Mears is sapped of his strength, suddenly all too cognizant of his own mortality. Perhaps due to the supernatural status of Barlow, perhaps due to the ferocity of Barlow's psychic monologue, perhaps due to Mears' own

1. Rice, *Interview with the Vampire*, 20.
2. King, *'Salem's Lot*, 388.

1

perceived human frailty, or perhaps a combination of all three, this devastating response to the manifestation of the vampire illustrates what theologian Rudolf Otto (1869–1937) described as the *mysterium tremendum*, "that is, a radically other mystery that brings on a stupefying combination of fascination and terror, wonder and dread,"[3] traits, Otto argued, of religious experience present in the sublime as well as the horrific. The feeling or presence of the *mysterium tremendum* occurs in response to the *numinous*, another term coined by Otto that describes encounters with a Divine occurrence, as well as a "feeling which remains where the concept fails."[4] The idea of the *numinous* is an ineffable one, impossible to label or explain in any tangible way. It is less an emotional response to a sacred presence and more a type of mindfulness, a fundamental understanding that one is faced with the hallowed, the Divine, or something wholly *other*.

The effectiveness of the vampire narrative (as well as the horror genre overall) relies on the awe and mystification brought on by the dread of the *mysterium tremendum* experienced in the wake of the supremacy of the *numinous* figure. Whether seen through the eyes of Ben Mears, Jonathan Harker from Bram Stoker's novel *Dracula*, or Charley Brewster in *Fright Night*, any of the heroes who have seen fit to directly challenge the supernatural presence and power of the vampire have been brought emotionally and spiritually low by the *numinous* presence of the undead, achieving a distinct and horrible awareness of their utter lack of ability to effectively act against the monster.

Not only is the vampire an ambiguity (*mysterium*) to those who encounter the creature, it possesses the ability to strike fear and trepidation (*tremendum*) in even the most heroic, emerging from the page and screen as an undoubtedly *numinous* figure. In the book *The Vampire as Numinous Experience: Spiritual Journeys with the Undead in British and American Literature*, Beth McDonald writes, "[I]t is not the degree or intensity of the fear that is most important, according to Otto; it is that the person not only trembles before something apparently absolute and powerful, but also that the person is left with a sense of the self's insignificance in relation to that absolute power."[5] Whether the *numinous* figure is benevolent or malevolent is not the issue. Rather, the witness to the *numinous* understands at a fundamental level that the mysterious figure, simply through its existence,

3. Beal, *Religion and Its Monsters*, 7.
4. Otto, *The Idea of the Holy*, xxi.
5. McDonald, *The Vampire as Numinous Experience*, 22.

poses an intrinsic danger to the accepted reality of the observer, creating an immediate sense of awe and, conceivably, horror that one's own humanity may not survive the encounter.

Interestingly, the concept of the *mysterium tremendum* put forth by Otto was meant to convey the effects of a distinctly religious encounter, a brush with the Divine or an agent thereof. Poole writes, "[R]eligious experience [is] a kind of horror movie, embodiments of the Divine that evoke feelings of terror. The monsters of the Bible are symbols of that horror."[6] As such, examining the vampire through the lens of the *mysterium tremendum* raises two very important questions: 1) If the vampire displays traits of the *numinous*, must we consider it a symbol of the Divine? Within the literary and cinematic mythology of the undead, the vampire has conquered death, promises everlasting life, and even displays power over certain aspects of the created order (e.g. the weather and nocturnal animals). 2) Is the presence of the Divine, for which the term *mysterium tremendum* was essentially coined, inherently horrific, even if essentially benevolent in nature?

Theology of Terror

Timothy Beal, addressing the overarching *modus operandi* of the literary work of H.P. Lovecraft, writes, "Lovecraft considered cosmic fear to be co-eval with religious experience, but he believed that modern religion (especially mainstream American Protestantism) had attuned itself exclusively to the more beneficent dimensions of cosmic mystery[.]"[7] In other words, mainstream Christianity chose to emphasize and promote the softer side of its religious heritage, explaining away, or simply outright disregarding, the darker topics of genocide, rape, filicide, etc. that are legion within the Judeo-Christian Scriptures. As a result, Lovecraft believed that the contemporary horror genre has emerged in its present form as a bifurcation to modern religion, a malevolent (although essential) compartment that the devout keep at arms length, while using it to compile their unspoken and unrealized fears about the shadow side of the Divine. Lovecraft wrote in his novella *The Call of Cthulhu*:

> The most merciful thing in the world . . . is the inability of the human mind to correlate all its contents. We live on a placid island

---

6. Poole, *Monsters in America*, 6.
7. Beal, *Religion and Its Monsters*, 181.

of ignorance in the midst of black seas of infinity, and it was not meant that we should voyage far . . . [S]ome day the piecing together of dissociated knowledge will open up such terrifying vistas of reality, and of our frightful position therein, that we shall either go mad from the revelation or flee from the deadly light into the peace and safety of a new dark age.[8]

The unspeakable reality of infinity that takes amorphous shape in the Lovecraftian mythos modeled in *The Call of Cthulhu* may in some ways reflect the equally indescribable and horrific elements of the Judeo-Christian God that have been knowingly obfuscated and shifted to the outright (and therefore easily marginalized and dismissed) genre of the monstrous. Both Christianity and the horror genre bear a striking resemblance, each filled with terrifying tales of inexplicable malevolence unleashed on humanity by way of unfathomable *numinous* entities who might manifest in the form of Dracula, the Great Old One Cthulhu, or the ancient deity Yahweh who, much like Cthulhu, takes very little issue with the death of hundreds of thousands, if not millions, of innocent people by way of floods and terrifying plagues.

The pages of both the Hebrew Bible and the New Testament are rife with the horrific, including cosmogonic chaos, mass murder (including the God ordained murder of children), worldwide disaster, demons, war, witchcraft, cannibalism, and the divinely endorsed exploits of Satan. However, this diabolic aspect of Scripture has either had its fangs dulled by the need for palatable and civilized religious practices, or ignored altogether by contemporary mainline communities of faith.[9] Through the avenue of the horror genre, however, particularly the traditional vampire narrative found in western literature and cinema, the monstrous has found an avenue to convey the power of its own religious experience, the horrific Divine found in the *mysterium tremendum*. Cowan discusses this at length:

> [I]t matters little whether Moses really met with Yahweh, whether the Ark really destroyed all who touched it, or whether sudden death came to those who entered the Holy of Holies unbidden by the Divine. The point is that they are remembered in the sacred narratives as though they really happened, and for hundreds of millions of Jews and Christians worldwide, they have behind them

8. Lovecraft, *The Call of Cthulhu*, 76.

9. This is not to say that the diabolic side of the Divine is entirely ignored by all faith communities, especially when said communities feel the need to condemn those they feel are living a life of sin.

the power of memory, mythistory, and, for some, literal truth . . .
The fact of the matter, however, is that fear (insert terror) is the
thread that often holds the cloth of religion together.[10]

Cowan's astute analysis finds illustrative life in the 1995 film *The
Prophecy*[11] when the angel Gabriel (Christopher Walken) leaves Heaven for
Earth in order to secure a weapon, a dark soul that would enable him to win
a second war in the heavenly realms. Standing in his way is Thomas Dagget
(Elias Koteas), a former priest who left his holy calling after suffering a
series of frightening visions of an eternity not necessarily defined by peace
never ending. Echoing the earlier passage from *The Call of Cthulhu* by H.P.
Lovecraft, at one point Daggett asks, "Some people lose their faith because
Heaven shows them too little. But how many people lose their faith because
Heaven showed them too much?"[12] Daggett goes on to wonder aloud:

> Did you ever notice how in the Bible, whenever God needed to
> punish someone, or make an example, or whenever God needed
> a killing, he sent an angel? Did you ever wonder what a creature
> like that must be like? A whole existence spent praising your God,
> but always with one wing dipped in blood. Would you ever really
> want to see an angel?[13]

Gabriel puts a definitive exclamation point on this query from Daggett
when he declares, "I'm an angel. I kill firstborns while their mamas watch. I
turn cities into salt. I even, when I feel like it, rip the souls from little girls,
and from now till kingdom come, the only thing you can count on in your
existence is never understanding why."[14]

Throughout the Hebrew Bible, figures such as Moses, Jacob, and Abraham are in some way confronted with the face of God through the *mysterium tremendum* embodied in the angelic, each encounter leaving profound
and life altering effects for those involved. For example, Adam and Eve were
prevented from ever reentering Paradise by an angel with a fiery sword, and
not only was the hometown of Lot destroyed after the arrival of two angels
in Sodom, he was also widowed as a result of his wife disobeying the angels
and glancing over her shoulder at the destruction behind her. Meanwhile,

10. Cowan, *Sacred Terror*, 51–52.
11. The film was interestingly renamed *God's Secret Army* in Europe.
12. *The Prophecy*, Widen, 1999.
13. Ibid., Widen.
14. Ibid., Widen.

angels are just as dangerous, if not more so, in the New Testament, beginning with Gabriel striking Zechariah mute for having the audacity to believe that he was too timeworn to father the baby that would ultimately become John the Baptist. And in the Apocalypse of John, angels, at the behest of the Divine, unleash unfathomable violence, death, and destruction upon the physical world, sounding trumpets of destruction, pouring out bowls of plague and death, and killing non-believers wholesale.

Indeed, the biblical precedent of the angel appears to be an immensely appropriate lens through which to examine the function and consequence of the undead. While the appearance of the vampire is, in fact, a human crust disguising a supernatural being, angelic appearances in the Hebrew Bible and New Testament served a similar role. Often in Scripture, the countenance of the angel is human, initially showing no traits of the *numinous*, as in Genesis 18 when three angelic guests appeared to Abraham, soon followed by the two angels visiting Sodom in nothing more than human facades. Similarly, in the traditional vampire narrative within popular culture, the vampire often appears to be just as human as members of the general community until the visage transforms into a horrific perversion of the created order. The typical response of the corporeal cast of characters to the *mysterium tremendum* of the vampire is indistinguishable from the typical response of the mortal to angels in Scripture: fear, awe, horror, and foreboding. In the novel *Vampire$* by John Steakley, a vampire suddenly appears amidst Team Crow, a grizzled and hardened group of accomplished and fearless Vampire Hunters. At night and without their weapons, the undead fiend quickly dispatches the group. Those few who are able to escape a violent death are left shaken, devastated, and weeping, brought to the fearful realization of their own mortality by the *numinous* power and presence of the vampire.

The response of the disciples to an apparently undead Jesus in the upper room bears a striking resemblance to that of Team Crow. "Jesus himself stood among them and said to them, 'Peace be with you.' They were startled and terrified, and thought that they were seeing a ghost."[15] By this account, while Jesus looked physically as he did before his death, his post-mortem appearance to the disciples created a horrific response, one not dissimilar to the ghastly disbelief of Quincey Morris (Bill Campbell), Jack Seward (Richard E. Grant), and Lord Arthur Holmwood (Cary Elwes) when faced

15. Luke 24:36–37 (NRSV).

with the undead Lucy Westenra (Sadie Frost) in Francis Ford Coppola's film *Bram Stoker's Dracula* (2002).

Never Understanding Why: The Horror of Job

Perhaps the greatest example within Scripture of the sway of *mysterium tremendum* as a result of theological terror would be through the narrative of Job, a biblical story that irrevocably colors all other scriptural narratives. It is through the story of Job that we are confronted by a painful and problematic lesson. Not in the holiness and significance of suffering, as has been imparted by Sunday school teachers from time immemorial, but in the capriciousness and unpredictability of Yahweh.

The horror to be found at the heart of the story of Job is the shocking ambivalence of the Divine, the promotion by God of violence and death, working with and through Satan[16] against a man allegedly favored by the Creator. In a theological world where pain was an indicator of a life out of sync with the precepts of God, the story of Job would have created confusion and fear in the faithful. The life of Job is entirely shattered in every conceivable manner, only to be rewarded throughout his terror and pain with the silence of God, echoing the chilling words of Gabriel from the film *The Prophecy*: "And from now till kingdom come, the only thing you can count on in your existence is never understanding why."

While the reader of the narrative knows that the travails of Job are the result of a wager between Satan and the Divine (as if that makes it acceptable), Job undoubtedly sees himself as cursed, suddenly cast from the favor of God to suffer the misery of the cosmos. It is important here to note how the vampire Barlow in *'Salem's Lot* closely echoes Job's exclamation of "Face me and be appalled"[17] when he commands Ben Mears, "Look upon me and despair!"[18] Both literary figures seem to be aware of the theological terror they are playing a vital role in, serving dualistically as a result and an example of the power of the *mysterium tremendum* at play within their existence. Beal writes:

> Job's embittered declaration "let there be darkness" is a literal inversion of God's own initial world-creative words . . . At this point

---

16. God basically acquiesces to a bet that Satan proposes, the equivalent of a cosmic pissing contest.

17. Job 21:5 (NRSV).

18. King, *'Salem's Lot*, 458.

in his summoning of chaos against cosmos, Job seeks the company of the chaos monsters Yam and Leviathan . . . Job *desires* them, even *identifies with* them, conjuring them as a destructive force against creation.[19]

Job setting his face against the Divine and aligning himself with chaos and darkness is an imaginative starting point for the development and emergence of the vampire, a motif embodied presciently in the film *Bram Stoker's Dracula*. At the start of the movie, a Romanian Christian knight, Draculea (Gary Oldman), leaves his bride Elisabeta (Winona Ryder) in order to lead his army into battle against the invading Muslim Turks. Draculea emerges victorious, kissing a crucifix and declaring, "God be praised! I am victorious!"[20] However, through a nefarious trick by the Turks, Elisabeta believes her husband to have died in battle and commits suicide by flinging herself into a river. Draculea arrives home to find her dead body surrounded by a cadre of priests in a chapel:

> BISHOP: She has taken her own life. Her soul cannot be saved. She is damned. It is God's Law.
>
> DRACULEA: Nooo! Is this my reward for defending God's church?
>
> BISHOP: Sacrilege!
>
> DRACULEA: I renounce God! I shall rise from my own death to avenge hers with all the powers of darkness![21]

Enraged, Draculea brandishes his sword and violently impales a large stone crucifix atop the chapel altar. Blood gushes forth out of the cross and Draculea snatches a chalice with which he fills with the blood and drinks from it. "The blood is the life," he says. "And it shall be mine."[22] Not only does Draculea invoke here a cosmogonic chaos of sorts, aligning himself with darkness in a rant reminiscent of Job ("Let there be darkness"), he also partakes of an inverted and perverted communion at the altar of Christ. As we have discussed, it is not difficult to see the connection between the Christian ritualistic consumption of the symbolic(?) blood of Jesus and the fictional consumption of blood by Dracula and his ilk. As Clements points out, this is more than likely intended to be "an inversion of this act

19. Beal, *Religion and Its Monsters*, 41 & 43.

20. *Bram Stoker's Dracula*, Coppola, 1992.

21. Ibid., Coppola.

22. Ibid., Coppola.

of Christian devotion,"[23] and should be taken as such, placing the vampire directly in the company of Job.

This inversion of communion is a theological horror, the horror of the vampire, and challenges the sacred order by seeking the solace of chaos as modeled by Job versus the face and order of the Divine. Dracula, as envisioned by Coppola, introduces a new communion, one directly opposed to the ritualistic intimacy modeled by Christ and introducing chaos into the sacred order. Cowan writes, "The advent of one unseen order heralds – or at least threatens – the disappearance of another."[24] Such a threat against the *status quo* instills terror across a wide spectrum of ideologies,[25] evidenced, for example, in the histrionics emerging from the white patriarchal establishment over Census Bureau projections of a white minority in the United States by 2043. In the case of Draculea, not only does his inversion of the established order surprise and horrify the attendant priests due to its visceral power of disgust, it is the genesis of a new order in defiance of the established one, signifying the vampire emerging directly out of the *mysterium tremendum*, as well as serving as an agent of it.

After the resurrection but before the ascendance into heaven of Jesus the Christ within the narrative of the Gospels, the Nazarene has plunged through the mortal coil of the organic order of life and death, straddling the invisible chasm between the two. Neither dead nor alive and inhabiting a realm that can only be described as undeath, the *numinous* aura of the Christian demigod is evident to all who bear witness to his post-crucifixion exploits. So it is with the vampire, a once human now transcendent figure that conquered death and offers the same freedom from the unassailable laws of God and nature. Granted, while the avenue of eternal life that Jesus provides promises a spiritual bounty of grace while the vampire seems to be one of darkness and evil, their respective *modus operandi* regarding salvation are too similar to dismiss.

If the vampire is indeed a figure of the *numinous*, displaying traits of the Divine while exhibiting the influence of *mysterium tremendum*, what can this transcendent fictional character tell us about God and the role the Divine plays in the structure and existence of evil? This question finds its

---

23. Clements, *Vampire Defanged*, 25.

24. Cowan, *Sacred Terror*, 67.

25. Fox News host Bill O'Reilly, during coverage of the 2012 presidential election, infamously asserted, "Obama wins because it's not a traditional America anymore. The white establishment is the minority. People want things."

roots in the story of Job and is carried into contemporary life through the engine of the vampire narrative. While the generally accepted view of the traditional western vampire is one of ultimate evil standing in opposition to the inherent righteousness of the Divine, the next several chapters will examine how the complexity of the mythology of the vampire in popular culture, as well as an honest analysis of the theologically problematic enigma of theodicy, may pose more demanding questions than hopeful answers.

2

Worship of the Blood God:
The Vampire as Agent of Theodicy

"So you know about the blood cult? The one that asks its
faithful to eat the body and drink the blood of its savior."[1]

—*PROFESSOR TANNER (JAKE BUSEY),*
FROM FROM DUSK TILL DAWN: THE SERIES

PERHAPS MOST EXPLICIT IN an analysis of what the vampire represents or symbolizes in literature and cinema is that of incarnate sin or evil. And thus, as so often ensues in a discussion of evil, the vampire is exposed as a catalyst for queries of theodicy, or why God allows evil to subsist in the created order. Cowan writes, "Why do we fear the chaogonic invasion/inversion of our world, and the apparent powerlessness (or capriciousness) of God in the face of it? In this sense, it is possible that cinematic horror is one cultural means by which we confront the classic theological problem of evil."[2] The vampire, as a courier of the horrific, brings to the fore in a dialogue of theodicy and sin a vital analysis of theological perspectives addressing the often-perceived ambivalence of the Divine in the face of evil.

Concerns, questions and debates over sin, evil, and theodicy have been grappled with by theologians and philosophers for millennia, and serve as the nucleus of the theological repercussions of the vampire as religious

---

1. *From Dusk Till Dawn: The Series.* "Mistress," March 24, 2014.
2. Cowan, *Sacred Terror,* 58.

narrative. As such, the vampire can effectively serve as a lens through which to ask those disquieting questions tucked away and slumbering in the religious shadows. Where is God amidst the three million children who die each year from starvation and malnutrition? How, if God is right and just, can the most wicked and greediest of humanity thrive while tens of millions suffer in disease, hunger, and poverty?[3] Justo L. González and Zaida Maldonado Pérez summarize the issue as such:

> The problems [with theodicy] is in the difficulty of affirming three points that seem to be mutually contradictory: (1) God is good; (2) God is all-powerful; (3) evil is real. Every solution that has been proposed throughout history simply ignores or minimizes one of these three points . . . that neither philosophers nor theologians nor even the Bible itself offer a satisfactory explanation of evil should not surprise us. What makes evil such is precisely that it interrupts the order, that it breaks all harmony, that it has neither reason nor explanation. Were we able to explain it, it would no longer be the powerful and overwhelming mystery of iniquity that it is.[4]

This disruption of the ordained order is at the core of the mythos of the vampire and of the concept of monsters across the spectrum. As will be illustrated, the vampire has often been portrayed, theologically, as a creature without "reason nor explanation," and serves as a prevailing agent of enticement too potent to oppose or, perhaps even worse, for God to prohibit. The Francis Ford Coppola iteration of the figure of Dracula achieves immortality through sheer force of will, defeating the natural created order in the hopes of achieving some level of revenge against the Almighty for the death of his wife.

Beal, while specifically discussing Mary Shelley's novel *Frankenstein*, nevertheless cuts to the foundation of the problem that the presence of the vampire exposes when he writes, "The voice of the monster is the audacious voice of theodicy. It is addressed not only to the creator Frankenstein but also to the creator God. Why did you make me? . . . What kind of Divine justice is this? What kind of God are you? The horror of Frankenstein is a profoundly theological horror."[5] This sentiment is echoed in the *numinous* shadow of the vampire. If, as Beal goes on to argue, the vampire "is a chaos

---

3. Oxfam International reported in early 2014 that the eighty-five richest people on the planet are worth as much as the poorest fifty percent of the world's population.

4. González and Pérez, *An Introduction to Christian Theology*, 70.

5. Beal, *Religion and Its Monsters*, 3.

monster who invades the divinely ordained order of the cosmos,"[6] then the vampire narrative presents an inimitable opportunity to discuss theories of sin, temptation, and even religious ethics that attempt to look beyond traditional and often distorted Christian definitions of good and evil.

As Jack Crow, Vampire Hunter and protagonist in the novel *Vampire$*, bemoans, "I know fucking well there's a God because I kill vampires for a living. Are you listening? I kill vampires for money . . . so don't tell me there ain't no God. I know fucking well there's a God. I just don't understand him."[7] This type of apologetic, based on the prickly association between God and evil, is echoed by Seth Gecko (George Clooney) in the film *From Dusk Till Dawn* (1996) when he declares, "I've always said that God can kiss my ass, but I just changed my lifetime tune about 10 minutes ago. Because I know that whatever is out there trying to get in is pure evil straight from Hell. And if there is a Hell and those sons of bitches are from it, then there has got to be a Heaven."[8] Gecko, a bank robber and murderer, colorfully illustrates that the vampire, by its very presence, is in some manner representing the existence of God.

The nature of the vampire narrative takes place in the borderland region between the natural and the supernatural, the undead figure consistently imbued with powers that, for all intents and purposes, are Divine in weight and scope. Physical transformation, the ability to corrupt the soul of the living, psychological dominion over mortals, and, most importantly, the ability to transcend and negate the authority of death are just a sampling of traits vampires have displayed in popular culture over the last century. Whether those powers are meant to indicate the work of God or Satan (or both), the result is the establishment of a distinctly religious icon.

Of course, many view the western vampire narrative in popular culture as a type of Christian parable established as a tool of proselytization through the medium of entertainment, a religious morality play by way of the "penny dreadful." As such, the vampire as a religious symbol is intended to move the reader or viewer toward the saving grace of God, serving as the foil to the heroic, right, and true nature of the Divine. Alas, the ideologies and philosophies of the monstrous and the holy often become hopelessly enmeshed, the awful (full of awe?) and the hallowed becoming indistinguishable from one another. As Beal asks, "Does *being* God end up being

6. Ibid., 134.

7. Steakley, *Vampire$*, 67.

8. *From Dusk Till Dawn*, Rodriguez, 1996.

monstrous? Who is more monstrous, the creature who must live through this vale of tears, or the creator who put them there?"[9]

We can see this ethical quandary played out in the debate surrounding American drone strikes in countries where the United States is not currently at war. Terrorism, that is the use of violence and intimidation by organizations in the pursuit of political goals, is a real and legitimate threat to the world, and requires unique strategies beyond traditional tactics of warfare on a large scale. That said, drone strikes in regions such as Pakistan kill, according to some estimates,[10] one legitimate terrorist for every fifty innocent victims. Some view these instances as acceptable cases of collateral damage, unfortunate by-products of the "war on terror" committed by an exceptional nation. However, similar to the question of when gods become monsters, when does a nation distort and eventually obliterate the line between justice and terror, displaying a ghastly ambivalence toward those innocent men, women, and children victimized by its actions?

Within Judeo-Christian Scripture, one is often confronted with a similarly disturbing ambivalence around the unique brew of violence, abhorrent sexual ethics, and misogyny that is not only endorsed by God, they are indistinguishable from the nature and agency of God. The horror of the ten plagues in the Hebrew scriptures, culminating in "the destroyer"[11] Yahweh murdering *en masse* the first born of Egypt, coupled with the apparent Divine rape of a fifteen-year-old girl named Mary within the New Testament,[12] should be sufficient to provide even the most faithful religious adherent concern as to how such behavior is anything but monstrous. These two examples, of which the Judeo-Christian scriptures are rife, are an uncomfortable miscegenation of the holy and the horrific, only made palatable through the thin pall of religious tradition and convoluted theological contortions.

These biblical accounts, along with our aforementioned foxhole theologians Jack Crow and Seth Gecko, are sharing in the philosophical and theological dilemma of theodicy. In the novel *The Last Temptation of Christ* by Nikos Kazantzakis, the character of Jesus observes, "Someone came. Surely it was God, God . . . or was it the devil? Who can tell them apart?

---

9. Beal, *Religion and Its Monsters*, 5.

10. According to a joint study released by Stanford and New York University: http://www.livingunderdrones.org/report/.

11. Exodus 12:23 (NRSV).

12. Some argue that Mary gives consent within the text.

They exchange faces; God sometimes becomes all darkness, the devil all light, and the mind of man is left in a muddle."[13] Crow, Gecko, and Kazantzakis' Jesus all ascertain that, while it might be innate to ask the question, "Where is God in evil," it is considered more menacing to ask, "Is God the cause of evil?"

In *The Strange Trial of Mr. Hyde: A New Look at the Nature of Human Evil*, Jungian psychoanalyst and Episcopal priest John Sanford contends, "The specific failure of Christianity is its failure to include the evil side of God in its understanding of the Divine nature."[14] In the Hebrew Bible, a general reading quickly reveals that Yahweh encompasses both good and evil, serving as the face of both the sublime and the terrible, the Creator of Genesis and the Destroyer of Exodus.

This troubling and discomforting exercise of questioning and/or blaming the Divine, both vehicles that carry us into excursions through the valley of theodicy, are unavoidable when discussing the theological implications of the vampire narrative. In *Strangers, Gods, and Monsters: Interpreting Otherness*, Richard Kearney addresses this riddle of evil in the divinely created order:

> While lament protests against evil that befalls us, blame locates evil within a moral agent. The former relates to something passively endured, the latter to something actively committed . . . The fact is, of course, that these twin categories are almost always intertwined in biblical accounts: in Genesis the serpent symbolizes an external focus of seduction but the fall signals Adam's own sense of *inner* culpability.[15]

The figure of the vampire, similar to the serpent in Scripture, often serves in the wider popular culture as the symbol of external focus of seduction that Kearney discusses. In the act of receiving or submitting to the vampire, the victim "feels guilty for committing a forbidden act while simultaneously experiencing invasion from an overwhelming force from without"[16] (e.g. Mina Harker, Louis de Pointe du Lac from *Interview with the Vampire*, etc.). In addition, similar to the serpent found in the Creation narrative, the vampire opens a window onto a myriad of theological inquiries. Within these narratives, what role does God play in generating,

13. Kazantzakis, *The Last Temptation of Christ*, 15.
14. Sanford, *The Strange Trial of Mr. Hyde*, 101.
15. Kearney, *Strangers, Gods, and Monsters*, 84.
16. Ibid., 84.

permitting, and promoting this cycle of temptation and iniquity? Does the vampire operate as a (super)natural evil or a moral evil? Or both? Does God support them or oppose them? Or does God even care? As we ask these questions using the vampire as the metaphoric lens, we are better able to grapple with and potentially subdue our concerns surrounding theodicy and the role of the Divine with regard to evil in the created order.

Stephen Asma, author of *On Monsters: An Unnatural History of Our Worst Fears*, writes, "Monsters became intertwined with the theological question, why did God create evil? One of the ways monsters were recast was as God's lackeys. Monsters threatened human health and happiness, but at God's bidding."[17] Asma here reverberates, albeit far more appropriately, the lament of both Jack Crow and Seth Gecko, both who seem to be articulating a warped and inverted apologetic for God while simultaneously questioning the character of God. Rather than, as the psalmist writes, "The heavens are telling the glory of God; and the firmament proclaims his handiwork,"[18] for Crow, Gecko, and Asma it is the survival of evil itself in the form of monsters that proclaims the existence of the Divine. Within their respective narratives, neither Crow nor Gecko experience a spiritual transformation whereby their lives become forever altered in the service of God. Rather, the Divine is simply acknowledged as a tool with which evil can be fought, even if that evil seems to flow from the very power they are relying on for protection.

Slaying the Dragon

In the epigraph found at the beginning of his novel *Coraline*, author Neil Gaiman paraphrases G.K. Chesterton with the quote, "Fairy tales are more than true — not because they tell us dragons exist, but because they tell us dragons can be beaten."[19] Monsters, whether emerging from tribal folklore, world mythology, or the Hebrew Bible, are summoned for the purpose of being defeated and destroyed, thereby affirming and solidifying the role of the righteous within the natural order. To this end, a normative dynamic of the vampire narrative is the trope of the Vampire Hunter, the hero or heroes who confront the malevolent supernatural invasion of the undead in defense of society and God. In the traditional western vampire mythos, the

17. Asma, *On Monsters*, 63.

18. Psalm 19:1–2 (NRSV).

19. Gaiman, *Coraline*, epigraph.

Vampire Hunter can often serve as the *de facto* apologist for the existence of the Divine as, through the various applied machineries of deliverance at their disposal, the monster falls, proving that righteousness, as opposed to evil, is the accepted order of creation. If viewed as a Christian allegory, the vampire within the narrative becomes a stand-in for Satan, thusly the power of God reigns supreme as the invasive demon is destroyed through the successful efforts of the Vampire Hunters.

However, this generally acknowledged assessment of the vampire narrative within popular culture fails to address, despite the vampire allegedly falling short in its bid to molest the created order of God, that evil still appears to be an integral, even divinely promoted, piece of that order. Illustrative of this is Behemoth and Leviathan, two monsters from the Hebrew Bible often seen as representing disorder and chaos and who seem to have an ambivalent relationship with Yahweh, a relationship that does not necessarily require their destruction. According to Asma:

> In some places, such as Psalm 74 and Job 3, Leviathan is described as a frightening monster that threatens order and stability . . . In some cases, God is described as smashing Leviathan's head, but in other places . . . Leviathan is identified as a part of God's wonderful creation . . . In these passages, the giant sea monster is an ally and even a manifestation of God.[20]

Asma brings the issue back to the original trilemma of theodicy described earlier in this book: (1) God is good; (2) God is all-powerful; (3) evil is real. From this theological algorithm logical questions arise, such as why God is portrayed in Scripture as actually reveling in the existence of monsters? And if God can easily dispatch monsters when they do get out of control, are the evil and metaphorical monsters in contemporary society "identified as a part of God's wonderful creation?" Is evil simply a manifestation of God? Should we not, in some way, be disturbed by the relationship between the Divine and the monsters at play within the Hebrew Bible?

In an article entitled "Religion and Vampires," S.T. Joshi asserts that vampires "may serve not only as an avatar of the Christian devil but as an avatar of divinity in general. The very nature of the vampire may cause it to stand as a theophany, a manifestation of the Divine."[21] In other words, the vampire may serve as a window into the nature of God with regard to the relationship the Divine maintains with evil. The mortal individual, when

20. Asma, *On Monsters*, 65–66.

21. Joshi, "Religion and Vampires," in *Encyclopedia of the Vampire*, 249.

faced with evil, demands to know where God is amidst the evil. The answer, however, might be as simple as God being represented *in* and *by* the evil, in much the same way that the monsters of the Hebrew Bible represented, in some respects, the dualistic and complicated nature of Yahweh.

With regard to the traditional vampire narrative in popular culture, a clearly Manichean system is established with the vampire standing in opposition to the Divine. That said, other than manifesting through the various sacred icons and applied machineries of deliverance available to the Vampire Hunter, God rarely sees fit to make an appearance within the various narratives. Considering the frightening stakes of spiritual oblivion at play within the vampire mythos, it is shocking to note how veiled the presence of God actually is, particularly within the storylines where the Christian allegorical strains are less than subtle. It would seem, time and again, that the omnipotent Creator has left the mortal protagonist with nothing more than assorted religious trinkets with which to do battle against ultimate evil.

All of this excavates an imperative theological question: If God can only address the dilemma of evil through the frailty of human agency, what must be assumed about the nature of God when said agency fails and the monster refuses to yield? In a strictly binary system of good and evil, is the implicit refusal of God to crush the head of Leviathan or Behemoth an admission of the complicity of God with regard to evil in the world? The traditional vampire narrative, commencing with *Dracula*, confronts the culture with this inconsistency.

Bram Stoker's classic novel (and the countless vampire narratives that emerged in its wake) is more than an entertaining and horrific yarn, it is our entry into a complex theological conversation about a God who gives license to countless authentic horrors, a Divine presence that both creates and destroys with equal capriciousness. For many, it is a dialogue that may find its foundation in the Job-like lament expressed by the swaggering Vampire Hunter Jack Crow when he snarls, "I know fucking well there's a God. I just don't understand him."

3

Take My Hand: The Vampire as Embodiment of Sin

"You will always be fond of me. I represent to you all the sins you never had the courage to commit."

—*LORD HENRY, FROM* THE PICTURE OF
DORIAN GRAY *BY OSCAR WILDE*[1]

DESPITE THE THEME OF the ambivalence of God at play within the western vampire narrative, in many respects the spiritual metaphor of the figure of the vampire succeeds at cutting to the essence of the theological problem of sin. Some scholars of religion, such as Regent University Associate Professor of English Susannah Clements, believe that the vampire is the fictional embodiment of sin. Throughout her book *The Vampire Defanged*, Clements subscribes to a common view of sin, one that turns theological turpitude into a personal preference, spiritualizing and privatizing it, transforming the power of sin into a catalog of insalubrious exploits. In the F. Paul Wilson novel *Midnight Mass*, this view of sin as a personal choice is reflected in a discussion between Catholic priest Father Joe and his friend Rabbi Zev, two survivors of a worldwide vampiric outbreak. Joe, struggling with his impotence as Christ's representative on Earth in the face of a wave of undead conversions, lashes out in righteous indignation:

1. Wilde, *The Picture of Dorian Grey*, 69.

"But Zev, we know there's some of the old personality left. I mean, they stay in their hometowns, usually in the basement of their old houses. They go after people they knew when they were alive. They're not just dumb predators, Zev. They've got the old consciousness they had when they were alive. Why can't they rise above it? Why can't they . . . resist?"

"Maybe the urge to feed is too strong to overcome?"

"Maybe. And maybe they just don't try hard enough."

"This is a hard line you're taking, my friend."[2]

What Father Joe is referencing, knowingly or not, is a commonly held Augustinian perception of sin (represented in the vampire) as a willing transgression of the accepted order, sin modeled as an ethical choice. Sin, however, "is something that separates humanity from God. Salvation is the break down of the barrier of separation between humanity and God . . . Sin is thus the antithesis of salvation."[3] Taken as such, sin is more an overall state of being and less a roadmap of unfortunate personal choices eventually leading to damnation. While the vampire in the novel *Midnight Mass* may indeed serve as a temptation for the mortal individual, *being* a vampire, or allowing oneself to become a vampire, is perceived and portrayed as a sinful act, one that should be resisted, ideally and most effectively through the various applied machineries of Christian deliverance. As the novel progresses, Father Joe is, in fact, turned into a vampire, and subsequently withstands the urge to give in to the evil nature of the fiend while still bound by the rules of the vampiric condition.[4]

For Clements, the vampire as embodiment of temptation and sin was never more explicit than in Bram Stoker's *Dracula*. She writes:

> *Dracula* is an explicitly Christian novel . . . Stoker builds his depiction of the vampire on a foundational Christian worldview, and that worldview shapes the formation of the vampire legend. By using the figure of the vampire as a representation of sin, temptation, and spiritual torment and by identifying the struggle against Dracula as a crusade against evil in the name of Jesus Christ[.][5]

2. Wilson, *Midnight Mass*, 81–82.
3. McGrath, *Theology*, 96–97.
4. Father Joe still needs blood to survive, sunlight harms him, etc.
5. Clements, *Vampire Defanged*, 9.

Clements argues vehemently that the literary figure of Dracula serves as a direct metaphor for sin, particularly sin as a knowing disobedience of the law. Throughout Bram Stoker's *Dracula*, the vampire often proves impossibly seductive to a number of characters, particularly for Jonathan Harker. Clements writes, "Harker is tantalized by the allure of sin, hypnotized into failing to fight against it, victimized and imprisoned by it, and finally threatened to death by it."[6] Clements asserts that Harker, who comes face-to-face with the overwhelming *mysterium tremendum* of the vampire, is found lacking in his resolve against the outward threat of sin represented in the figure of the undead Count and his brides. Author Kirk Schneider writes in his book *Horror and the Holy: Wisdom Teachings of the Monster Tale*:

> *Dracula* is a study of one side of infinity or the holy. It is a dizzying journey into concealment, seduction, and obliteration. At first we are captivated, even enchanted, by these conditions. Harker, for example, is stunned by the "beauty" of Dracula's terrain and finds its legends "interesting." Yet the deeper Harker probes, the greater is his dismay. Dracula's terrain is *too* exotic. His powers are *excessively* subtle.[7]

This view of temptation and sin as a kind of spiritual fly-paper, luring complicit victims into a deadly trap with promises of forbidden pleasure and earthly satisfaction, showcases the power of sin and the seemingly willing ineffectiveness of the individual, perhaps even God, to thwart it. There are countless examples in popular culture of men and women succumbing to the powers of the vampire, some willingly, some entranced, but all unable to resist. Schneider continues to discuss the effects of the sinful allure of the vampire on Jonathan Harker when he writes:

> Surrender is highlighted by Harker's submission to — and occasional fascination with — the Count. From the outset Harker loses strength ("sinks"), grows isolated ("lonely," "chilled"), and becomes trapped ("encircled by doom," "hemmed in by wolves"). He feels increasingly victimized ("hypnotized," entranced, dominated) by the Count and his "assistants." He grows dependent on them, feels he has no choice but to accept what they present to him, and becomes despondent.[8]

---

6. Ibid., 21.
7. Schneider, *Horror and the Holy*, 29.
8. Ibid., 21.

This motif is reflected time and again in vampire narratives apart from *Dracula*. Illustrative of this is the film *Fright Night* in which vampire Jerry Dandridge corners Edward (Stephen Geoffreys) in an alleyway. As Edward[9] cowers in fear, Jerry empathetically looks down on him and says, "You don't have to be afraid of me. I know what it's like being different. Only they won't pick on you anymore. Or beat you up. I'll see to that. All you have to do is take my hand."[10] Jerry then reaches out, revealing elongated fingers and sharp nails as Edward, obviously aware of the mortal danger he is in, willingly accepts the hand of the vampire.

This keen acquiescence to temptation is again illustrated in *Fright Night* when Amy (Amanda Bearse) is seduced by Jerry and eagerly removes her dress so that he might sink his fangs deep into her neck. It should be noted, however, that Amy is under some type of trance (a common trope within the vampire narrative), which arguably may have some effect on her agency and ability to resist. The same cannot be said of Edward.

The seduction of Evil Ed in *Fright Night* is most noticeably an echo of a conversation between Barlow,[11] the master vampire in Stephen King's *Salem's Lot,* and Dud Rogers, the humpbacked caretaker of the town dump in Jerusalem's Lot. Barlow, inquiring as to the deformity that Dud lives with, asks:

> "Does it perhaps inconvenience you in other ways?"
>
> "Well . . . girls . . . you know, girls . . . "
>
> "Of course," the old party said soothingly. "The girls laugh at you, do they not? They have no knowing of your manhood. Of your strength."
>
> "That's right," Dud whispered. "They laugh. *She* laughs."
>
> "Who is she?"
>
> "Ruthie Crockett. She . . . she . . . " The thought flew away. He let it. It didn't matter. Nothing mattered except this peace. This cool and complete peace.

---

9. Edward is unsympathetically referred to as Evil Ed by other students.

10. Holland, 1985.

11. The vampire Barlow in the novel differs drastically from his on-screen representation in the mini-series *'Salem's Lot*. In the book, he is intelligent and aristocratic, where the television show portrays him as a voiceless monster, with a look that mirrors Count Orlok from the film *Nosferatu*. The more human attributes of Barlow are given to the character of Straker, played with a reluctant menace by legendary actor James Mason.

"She makes the jokes perhaps? Snickers behind her hand? Nudges her friends when you pass?"

"Yes . . . "

"You shall have her. I am sure of it."

There was something . . . pleasant about this. Far away he seemed to hear sweet voices singing foul words. Silver chimes . . . white faces . . . Ruthie Crockett's voice . . . It was like drowning. Drowning in the old man's red-rimmed eyes.[12]

While some might rightfully squabble over these particular examples of vampiric casualties being the direct result of the influence of some type of mental jurisdiction or vampiric hypnosis, it might be argued that hypnosis is nothing more than the power of suggestion, as reflected in the exchange between Eve and the snake in the Genesis narrative:

Now the serpent was more crafty than any other wild animal that the Lord God had made. He said to the woman, "Did God say, 'You shall not eat from any tree in the garden'?" The woman said to the serpent, "We may eat of the fruit of the trees in the garden; but God said, 'You shall not eat of the fruit of the tree that is in the middle of the garden, nor shall you touch it, or you shall die.'" But the serpent said to the woman, "You will not die; for God knows that when you eat of it your eyes will be opened, and you will be like God, knowing good and evil." So when the woman saw that the tree was good for food, and that it was a delight to the eyes, and that the tree was to be desired to make one wise, she took of its fruit and ate; and she also gave some to her husband, who was with her, and he ate.[13]

Ultimately, no matter the strength of the argument presented by the serpent, Eve had to decide for herself whether or not to eat from the tree at the center of Paradise. However, does this independent agency exist for those unfortunate enough to be confronted by the *numinous* presence of the vampire? Here we encounter a significant problem of using the vampire as an allegory or symbol of sin and temptation, one that will be examined at greater length later in this book. Within the vampire narratives we have discussed thus far, what had any of the human characters done of their own volition to be consigned to such horrific circumstances?

12. King, *'Salem's Lot*, 145.
13. Genesis 3:1–6 (NRSV).

The Clarity of Evil

The overt representation of the vampire as the embodiment of sin is reflected in the plethora of Dracula-themed films produced by the British film corporation Hammer Studios in the 1950s through to the 1970s. There is very little nuance or gradation of ethics or ideology at work in these classic films, as the vampire is unabashedly evil, a supernatural threat to the created order. Contrastingly, the unseen presence of God and Jesus, represented in the various sacred icons and applied machineries of deliverance, is the primary weapon by which the Vampire Hunter is able to conquer Dracula and his assorted undead minions. Victims within these movies only become so inasmuch as their moral and religious fiber fails them, a reflection on their poor choices and not on any weakening of Divine power.

This view of Christian theology, easily traced to Bram Stoker's *Dracula*, is a distinctly Augustinian perspective, emphasizing two aspects of the human fallen state. Put simply, capital 'S' Sin refers to the fallen condition of humanity. Little 's' sin refers to the various individual acts one can either choose to partake in or struggle to oppose, illustrating the concept of free will. Tyron Inbody, writing in his book *The Transforming God: An Interpretation of Suffering and Evil*, elaborates: "[Augustine] attributes all evil, both natural and moral, directly or indirectly to the wrong choices of free rational creatures. All suffering and evil are attributable in their origin to sin and its penalty . . . [The] disobedience of Adam and Eve was a free act of will; that is it was not coerced by anyone else, including God."[14] The dilemma that is faced when blame is lifted from the Divine, at least in the case of the Genesis myth, is one of origins. If the serpent was created by God for the purpose of tempting Adam and Eve as a part of some cosmic experiment (eventually culminating in the death of God's own son), shouldn't Yahweh accept the blame for Original Sin? And if the serpent, perhaps created by a hand other than the Divine, is operating within the created order as a demonic antagonist, is God truly the omnipotent force we have been taught?

While the vampire embodies these muddy theological riddles, Terence Fisher, director of many of the vampire films from Hammer Studios, seems to disregard them entirely, opting for a more Manichean ideology, a clearly outlined conflict where the structure and ramifications are unambiguous. This desire to clearly delineate sides of sin and righteousness is also reflected in Father Callahan, a spiritually ambivalent priest within the

---

14. Inbody, *The Transforming God*, 40.

novel *'Salem's Lot*, who yearns for a world where foggy moral grays would disperse into clearly distinguished arenas of black and white:

> He wanted to see EVIL with it cerements of deception cast aside, with every feature of its visage clear. He wanted to slug it out toe to toe with EVIL . . . But there were no battles. There were only skirmishes of vague resolution. And EVIL did not wear one face but many, and all of them were vacuous and more often than not the chin was slicked with drool.[15]

The clarity of Evil that Father Callahan actively hopes for not only manifests itself later in *'Salem's Lot*, it is used as a selling point in the novel *Vampire$* when Jack Crow, seeking to draft a new member onto his team of Vampire Hunters, exclaims, "Don't you feel it? You're about to go fight evil. Real live goddamned evil. The real stuff. You get to fight for the good side. How many people ever get a chance to do that?"[16] Crow's rallying cry is not altogether different from the moralistic and theological demagoguery of the George W. Bush Administration leading up to the Iraq War and, more recently, the zealous religious rhetoric expressed by the nation of Israel in defense of the overwhelming violence they have inflicted upon the State of Palestine, rhetoric that seeks to paint the enemy as wholly other, embodying the traits of all that we fear and hate.

This clearly demarcated confrontation of good versus evil (or the appearance of it) is actively manifested in the various Hammer films directed by Fisher. With little abstruseness, Dracula (Christopher Lee) operates as a type of anti-Christ in opposition to Van Helsing (Peter Cushing), who serves as the righteous ambassador of God. Hallab writes, "A surprising number of vampire fictions recreate this combat myth with the aim of promoting Christian faith . . . These works usually abound in Christian references and allusions to make the point almost embarrassingly clear . . . The vampire's role is partly to illustrate the unmitigated evil of defying God's laws."[17] And, perhaps more frightening, the individual who chooses to defy those laws, who succumbs to the the vampire, must be destroyed in order to affirm the surety and righteousness of those laws, reflecting a frightening ethos of legalism more akin to the burning of witches and the stoning of adulteresses.

By modeling the arcane combination of the horrific and sublime, inhabiting the same rarified transcendent domain as the risen yet not

15. King, *'Salem's Lot*, 148.
16. Steakley, *Vampire$*, 104.
17. Hallab, *Vampire God*, 96.

ascended Jesus, and offering a blood ritual that promises the glory of a new life, the vampire represents a dreadful confrontation between good and evil, two sides of the same metaphorical coin proportionately set against each other with the fragility of human agency providing the determining factor. While Satan has traditionally assumed this adversarial role in Christian mythology and dogma, providing Christianity throughout history with a classic boogeyman and scapegoat, the vampire has come to represent this idea in modern narratives within western popular culture. The view of God as entirely virtuous paves the way for an equally contrasting influence within the narrative. John Carpenter's 1987 film *Prince of Darkness*, in which a group of graduate students in theoretical physics converge on a condemned church in Los Angeles to study what appears to be the physical manifestation of the anti-Christ, deals with many fascinating metaphysical and theological concepts,[18] not the least of which is the gaping orifice of darkness left by the existence of a pure God of light. And if nature truly does abhor a vacuum, this theoretical cavity would logically be occupied by the necessary existence of a mirror image: an anti-God.

In addition, by presenting within his films the vampire as an independent evil, one separate of the regulations of a God-ordered cosmos, Terence Fisher seems to leave open the opportunity for Evil to ultimately win. Similar to the influence of the serpent, who was seemingly acting with independent agency in the Garden of Eden, we see within the symbol of the vampire an uncanny ability to damn even the most innocent of souls, evident in the scorching of the forehead of Mina Harker by the holy wafer brandished by Van Helsing in Bram Stoker's novel *Dracula*, or the inability of Father Callahan to enter his very own church building in Stephen King's *'Salem's Lot*, or the fiery immolation of Virginia brought on by exposure to the sun in John Ajvide Lindqvist's book *Let the Right One In*. In addition, while Dracula suffers a form of defeat, he is inevitably resurrected at the commencement of each successive film (most notably in the Hammer films of Fisher), his malevolence and wickedness more pronounced than previous outings.

18. John Carpenter, writing the script under the pseudonym Martin Quatermass, provides some fascinating dialogue in the film with regard to religion, theology, and theoretical physics, exemplified by the character Professor Birack (Victor Wong): "From Job's friends insisting that the good are rewarded and the wicked punished, to the scientists of the 1930s proving to their horror the theorem that not everything can be proved, we've sought to impose order on the universe. But we've discovered something very surprising: while order DOES exist in the universe, it is not at all what we had in mind! Say goodbye to classical reality, because our logic collapses on the subatomic level into ghosts and shadows."

This all lends further credence to the ongoing proposition that the vampire (or the serpent, or Satan, or the anti-Christ, etc.) either stands apart from God's created order with equal power and agency, or is a vital part of that order, embodying the malevolent traits of a mercurial Divine presence. Either way, the tradition of the vampire narrative makes clear that the undead figure serves as an effective foil to an absent God, a God that is seemingly content with allowing the limitations of fallible humanity to dictate an imperfect and generally unpleasant outcome to events.

Feminist Icon?

While Fisher paints a Manichean view of Christian theology where pure evil is represented by Dracula and the power of righteousness is epitomized in Van Helsing, an enduring element of the Hammer films is ultimately the allure of vampiric temptation and the negative effects that yielding to sin have on the human condition. In some manner, Fisher's cinematic contributions to the vampire mythos would serve just as powerfully in a Sunday morning Christian worship service (minus the abundant cleavage), existing as they do as barely camouflaged filmic tracts of religious salvation, and the impossibility of an individual to resist the charisma of sin without the power of God in the form of Jesus Christ.

In the book *Terence Fisher: Horror, Myth and Religion*, author Paul Leggett examines at length the overtly religious message of the peril and seductiveness of vampiric iniquity that Fisher obsesses over within his work for Hammer. "Much has been made of the obvious anticipation and delight of Dracula's female victims in Fisher's films . . . Dracula's female victims enjoy being attacked. [In *The Horror of Dracula* (1958)] Lucy [Carol Marsh] prepares herself almost as a ritual sacrifice, laying herself out on the bed, arms extended, looking longingly at the door through which Dracula will enter."[19] For Fisher, it is important to illustrate the willingness and complicity that victims share in their succumbing to vampiric temptation. In both traditional folklore and narratives out of popular culture, an individual generally must invite a vampire into a house, negating the safe and sacred space that a home traditionally represents. Therefore, in Fisher's undead universe, while an individual may appear to be a victim, he or she is anything but a passive agent.

19. Leggett, *Terence Fisher: Horror, Myth and Religion*, 51, 53.

In his film *Dracula: Prince of Darkness* (1966), Fisher delves deeper into the corrupting effects of the power of sin. Helen (Barbara Shelley), a proper and rather prudish woman, is seduced by Dracula and ultimately transformed into a powerful and sexually unconcealed vampire. Leggett writes, "Whatever lustful origin may have existed in Helen's repressed nature has by now been totally dominated by Dracula's demonic influence. The writhing, screeching figure at the end bears no resemblance to the original Helen. In theological terms, sin has totally defaced Helen's humanity[.]"[20] While the overriding issue established by Fisher within his oeuvre is the unavoidable power of sin, an effective case could be made that such depictions of women as vampires serve to epitomize a latent fear of female empowerment in a patriarchal society. This fear reaches a zenith in the Hammer film *The Vampire Lovers* (1970), directed by Roy Ward Baker and based on the novella *Carmilla* by Sheridan Le Fanu, an unsubtle screed warning of the dangers inherent within female agency, particularly when that freedom leads a woman entirely out of patriarchal control in the form of a same-sex relationship. This concern over feminine agency is compounded when Carmilla, from the perspective of the patriarchy, seeks to seduce, convert, and indoctrinate other women and young girls into her lifestyle. The solution to such cultural insolence becomes, as demonstrated at the end of the story, the destruction of the undead instigator by driving a stake through her heart, bringing an end to the efforts of the vampire at transforming the strictly male-dominated culture.

In addition, echoes of the transformation of Helen in Fisher's *The Dracula: Prince of Darkness* can be found in the film *Fright Night*. Evil Ed and Amy experience both an outward physical transformation and a type of spiritual or emotional liberation. Shy and timid Edward is now powerful and beastly (as represented in his transformation into a wolf), and Amy evolves into a hypersexual woman. It would seem that, to some extent, the message within these narratives is not the danger of sin as it relates to the corruption of the soul, but the danger of sin as an impetus for shattering the conventions and expectations placed upon women within a male dominated society.

Pertinent to this issue of gender and sexual politics at play within the popular vampire narrative is the ancient Lilith myth, a Jewish legend that has found its most common telling in the *Alphabet of Ben Sira* from the ninth century. Briefly summarized, Lilith was created by God as the first

20. Ibid., 74.

wife of Adam. However, as she rightfully viewed herself on equal footing to that of her husband, Lilith refused to take the submissive role in their sexual copulations. This did not sit well with Adam, and Lilith fled Eden in order to live independently. Yahweh eventually demanded that she return and sent angels to secure her homecoming. She refused, even when threatened with death. David Leeming and Jake Page write in their book *Goddess: Myths of the Female Divine:*

> It came to be said of [Lilith] that, in her distant home, she coupled indiscriminately with demons and gave birth to legions of new demons, the *lilim*, who would haunt righteous men for millennia—she-demons, night-hags with flowing hair and feet that were claws who would slip into the beds of sleeping men and, squatting over them, copulate with them as they dreamed, milking them of their life force.[21]

This view of Lilith, reinforced in the book of Isaiah, elucidates her as a vampiric beast seeking to devour men and children, a cultural attempt by patriarchy to demonize the idea of a woman operating apart from, or even expressing dominance over, a male-centered hierarchy. In addition, the Lilith legend weaves a fascinating tapestry of a woman open about her sexuality and the power it affords her, and one who seeks agency in determining when and how that influence and eroticism is expressed. As such, the Lilith narrative has found a foothold in the larger vampire mythos within popular culture.

In the film *Tales From the Crypt: Bordello of Blood* (1996), Angie Everhart plays Lilith as a master vampire who runs a brothel where customers soon become dinner,[22] only to be thwarted by comedian and Fox News talking head Dennis Miller. Mia Kirshner embodied Lilith in the 2010 film *30 Days of Night: Dark Days* where she is described as the queen of the vampires. And most recently, the figure of Lilith, portrayed by actress Jessica Clark, featured prominently in the fifth and sixth seasons of the HBO series *True Blood* wherein she is revealed as the first of all vampires, created in God's image (who is also a vampire).

---

21. Leeming and Page, *Goddess: Myths of the Female Divine*, 113.

22. That same year, the film *From Dusk Till Dawn* shared a similar plot element, as patrons of the The Titty Twister bar find themselves battling strippers turned vampires led by a female master.

While many contemporary midrashim[23] of Lilith and the *Alphabet of Ben Sira* seek to re-imagine the myth as a feminist clarion call (which it very well can be), Lilith is, for all intents and purposes, written as a warning to the broad and pervasive patriarchal hierarchy of the dangers of the independent and sexually liberated woman. This viewpoint has actually been perpetuated in modern popular culture through the traditional vampire narrative. This continuing cultural dynamic not only strongly echoes the *Alphabet of Ben Sira* and the retelling of the Lilith legend, it plainly illustrates the ongoing stranglehold patriarchy has on society as a whole with regard to views of gender roles, responsibilities, and hierarchy. This was made disturbingly clear in the unanimous Republican rejection of the 2014 Paycheck Fairness Act where the United States Senate was unable to pass legislation that would have secured the right to equal pay for equal work for women.[24]

It would be a mistake to overlook or downplay the misogynistic and sexist overtones at work within the various vampire narratives that consistently promote the notion that women are more susceptible to sin than men.[25] Within the novel *Dracula*, many scholars have pointed out that we witness a consistent theme of a depraved and foreign sexuality, embodied in the vampire threatening the virtue of England's women, only to be destroyed by the desperate patriarchy determined to maintain societal norms. This motif, that of the spiritually defenseless female needing protection from invasive evil behind the shield of the "sacred" masculine, arguably originated in Bram Stoker's classic tale and found resonance in the vampire narratives thereafter. This is reflected throughout Stephen King's novel *'Salem's Lot* with its all-male contingent of Vampire Hunters, as well as in *Fright Night*, with Charley Brewster and Peter Vincent battling vampiric evil in the hope of rescuing Amy, the chaste love interest. However, it is the character of Mina Harker in *Dracula* that truly embodies the eagerness of the institution of patriarchy to maintain dominance over the accepted societal (and perceived natural) order and placing the male above the influence of evil and sin.

While Mina's then fiancé Jonathan was trapped and enticed by Dracula early in the novel, he was able, through the strength of his own (male?)

23. A process for interpreting biblical stories.

24. According to the United States Census Bureau, as recently as 2012 women who worked full time earned only seventy-seven cents for every dollar men earned.

25. Terence Fisher may have been referencing within his films a patriarchal view of the Genesis mythology as well as the apparent misogyny present in the Bram Stoker vampire opus *Dracula*.

agency, to resist and ultimately escape the clutches of the Count. Mina, however, having partaken in the unholy blood communion of Dracula, had been contaminated by evil (as evidenced by her being singed by a communion wafer) and has no power of her own to ultimately decide her own fate, whether theologically or relationally.[26]

In Francis Ford Coppola's film version of *Bram Stoker's Dracula*, the presence of the vampire in England seems to give rise to out of control passion and unfettered prurience in the female characters, threatening the prim and appropriate parameters laid out for them by a male dominated society. Mina in particular is imbued with a sense of strength and independence and makes the choice to be with Dracula. In the end, however, Mina is "saved" from the physical and spiritual clutches of Dracula, only to be transferred back into her role as a subservient woman, begging the question of whether it is the sin the vampire represents or the potential deconstruction of the patriarchal power structure that is to be feared? Ultimately, such a radical agent of change must be marginalized as malevolent, as sinful, and thus be destroyed at all costs.

26. Interestingly, in the silent film *Nosferatu* (which itself is a rough adaptation of *Bram Stoker's Dracula*), it is Ellen, modeled after Mina Harker, who sacrifices herself and alone slays the vampire by allowing Count Orlok to drink her blood. He becomes so distracted that he does not notice the sun rising until it is too late and he disintegrates.

4

"Propaganda": Christian Iconography in the Traditional Vampire Narrative

"We are symbols, and inhabit symbols."

—*FROM* THE POET *BY RALPH WALDO EMERSON*

TOWARD THE CONCLUSION OF the novel *Salem's Lot*, Father Callahan and Mark Petrie have suddenly and unexpectedly come face-to-face with Barlow, the master vampire well on his way to enslaving the town of Jerusalem's Lot.

> "And here you are!" Barlow had boomed good-naturedly in his rich, powerful voice. Mark attacked without thought and was captured instantly.
>
> Callahan moved forward, holding his cross up.
>
> Barlow's grin of triumph was instantly transformed into a rictus of agony. He fell back toward the sink, dragging the boy in front of him. Their feet crunched in the broken glass.
>
> "In God's name-" Callahan began.
>
> At the name of the Deity, Barlow screamed aloud as if he had been struck by a whip, his mouth open in a downward grimace, the needle fangs glimmering within.[1]

---

1. King, *'Salem's Lot*, 333.

Effectively illustrated in this scene is a common element of the traditional vampire narrative within popular culture, that is the cross of Christ being used as the primary weapon in the war against the undead. This classic trope found origin in Bram Stoker's *Dracula* and remained entrenched within the established mythology of the vampire for the next hundred years. Susannah Clements writes, "In Dracula, the power of the Christian cross is more than simply a plot device. The cross is a picture of one of the central themes of the novel, and it points to the way Stoker portrays the figure of the vampire."[2] For Clements, Count Dracula is not just a narrative figure with slight theological implications, she views Stoker's novel, and the vampire narrative as a whole, as a direct Christian allegory bound up in a spiritual morality play where God ultimately defeats the power of sin and death. From Stoker's novel to its filmic progeny as a classic Universal monster; from the vampires of the Hammer universe to their tongue-in-cheek homage in *Fright Night*; and from Stephen King's *'Salem's Lot* to its literary descendant in F. Paul Wilson's *Midnight Mass*; floating on the surface of these narratives is the undeniable sheen of Christian supremacy as, repeatedly, the vampire rises, stalks, victimizes, and is put down by the forces of good brandishing holy weaponry. Clements continues, "The cross and the figure of the vampire in Dracula are inextricably linked. Once the cross has been understood theologically in the context of the novel, then the vampire must be as well. The vampire — primarily Count Dracula himself — represents all of the forces that the cross must defeat."[3]

The film *Dracula 2000* is a rare contemporary cinematic attempt at explaining exactly why the assorted Christian icons and objects of salvation are able to impair Dracula (Gerard Butler) without secularizing the intrinsic religious subtext behind them. In the movie, the Count, surviving into the turn of the twenty-first century, pursues Mary (Justine Waddell), a distant relative of his arch-nemesis Abraham Van Helsing (Christopher Plummer), while also concealing the surprising origin of his existence; he is the embodiment of the legendary betrayer Judas Iscariot, now cursed to live a perverted form of the eternal life that Jesus promised him. As such, Judas, now Dracula, has a slight aversion to all things holy.[4]

2. Clements, *Vampire Defanged*, 14.

3. Ibid., 16.

4. Other entertainment mediums have played with this theme, such as the Christian novel *The Last Confession of the Vampire Judas Iscariot* (Köehler Books), while some narratives, such as the fairly entertaining *Blood of the Lamb: A Novel of Secrets* (Signet Publishing) have painted Jesus himself as a vampire. Most entertaining, perhaps, is the

While *Dracula 2000* succeeds at providing a particularly fascinating and imaginative perspective on the Dracula mythos, it also serves as an excellent sketch of the apparent, although often unspoken, limitations of the various sacred icons associated with the downfall of the vampire. At one point in the film, a priest (Nathan Fillion) brandishes a Christian Bible against Dracula, its pages exploding outward in a ferocious and fiery surge. The holy book, a sacred armament in the presence of the undead, has little effect on the vampire who smirks and mutters, "Propaganda."[5]

In addition, in *Dracula 2000* the crucifix has a limited effect on Dracula (even as he hangs beneath one at the climax of the film, the tacky neon bordered face of Jesus smiling down on him), much in the same way the cross contains limited potency for the Vampire Hunters in Bram Stoker's novel *Dracula*. Professor Van Helsing, Harker et al. are left with only Divine half measures, as the symbols of the holy only provisionally repel the vampire rather than destroy it. In Francis Ford Coppola's *Bram Stoker's Dracula*, one of the vampire brides causes the crucifix hanging from the neck of Jonathan Harker (Keanu Reeves) to melt, seductively licking the spot on his skin where it once inhabited. In addition, when confronting Dracula after his seduction of Mina Murray, the cross that is wielded by Van Helsing (Anthony Hopkins) bursts into flames as the eccentric doctor is forced to cast it aside.

In some sense, the filmgoer viewing *Dracula 2000* or *Bram Stoker's Dracula* might be left less with the impression of the authority of Christianity and more the impotency of a faith that fails in the face of evil, necessitating the use of physical strength by its followers as a result of that failure, which would lead us through the disturbing portal of seeking redemption through violence, often the last recourse of the religious zealot with regard to efforts at proselytization and conversion.

If we return to the terrifying scene of Father Callahan facing off with Barlow in *'Salem's Lot*, we are witness to a vampire held at bay by the power of the cross of Christ, though most assuredly not defeated by it. Barlow, having captured Mark Petrie, agrees to let the boy go if Callahan will cast his cross aside and face the master vampire one-on-one.

> Callahan stood indecisive. Why throw it down? Drive him off, settle for a draw tonight, and tomorrow —

2001 low budget film *Jesus Christ Vampire Hunter,* where the Messiah must team with lucha libre wrestling legend El Santos to battle vampire hordes.

5. *Dracula 2000*, Lussier, 2000.

But a deeper part of his mind warned. To deny the vampire's challenge was to risk possibilities far graver than any he had considered. If he dared not throw the cross aside, it would be as much as admitting . . . admitting . . . what? If only things weren't going so fast, if one only had time to think, to reason it out —
The cross's glow was dying . . . Barlow reached from the darkness and plucked the cross from his fingers. Callahan cried out miserably . . . and the next sound would haunt him for the rest of his life: two dry snaps as Barlow broke the arms of the cross, and a meaningless thump as he threw it on the floor.[6]

Barlow goes on to admonish Callahan over his lack of faith in the very power he purportedly serves. "You have forgotten the doctrine of your own church, is it not so? The cross . . . the bread and wine . . . the confessional . . . only symbols. Without faith, the cross is only wood, the bread baked wheat, the wine sour grapes. If you had cast the cross away, you should have beaten me another night."[7]

This chilling scene is also echoed in *Hellraiser III: Hell On Earth* (1992). While not a vampire narrative, Cowan points out how the demonic villain Pinhead stalks a victim through a large Catholic Church, only to be confronted by an angry priest. He writes, "The priest holds up a crucifix, shouting, 'How dare you?' But, because even demons can quote Scripture, Pinhead replies, 'Thou shalt not bow down before any graven image,' and the heavy metal cross melts in the cleric's hand."[8]

A similar scene is played out in the film *Fright Night* when Peter Vincent and Charley Brewster confront the vampire Jerry Dandridge. Brandishing the cross of Christ, Vincent thrusts the icon toward Dandridge and commands, somewhat melodramatically, "Stop! You creature of the night!" The vampire joyfully laughs, then nonchalantly reaches out, snatches the cross, and crushes it, explaining, "You have to have faith for this to work on me, Mr. Vincent."[9]

Both the vampiric figures of Barlow and Dandridge seem to indicate that the crucifix itself is not the actual weapon used against the vampire, it is within the indefinable locus of faith where the power is rightly manifested, faith translated through the image of the cross of Christ. As such, it would seem that the faith of most Vampire Hunters is lacking, as the vampire is

6. King, *'Salem's Lot*, 336–337.
7. Ibid., 337.
8. Cowan, *Sacred Terror*, 88.
9. Holland, 1985.

rarely, if ever, defeated solely by the cross, holy water, wafer etc., but by the violent rupturing of flesh and bone courtesy of a wooden stake. Clements writes, "It takes faith to begin to fight against the forces of evil . . . and the faith that ultimately saves is a faith in God's power."[10] However, rather than these scenes instilling comfort in the presence and authority of God, perhaps these (and countless other) cultural examples of the applied machineries of deliverance displaying such ineffectual power might draw stark attention to the problem of symbols of the Divine diluting the supernatural influence said symbols are substituting for, thus adversely affecting the faith of the believer in the face of the vampire. Philosopher Jean Baudrillard encompasses this issue within his discussion of what he calls *simulacra*:[11]

> But what becomes of the divinity when it reveals itself in icons, when it is multiplied in simulacra? Does it remain the supreme power that is simply incarnated in images as a visible theology? Or does it volatilize itself in the simulacra that, alone, deploy their power and pomp of fascination — the visible machinery of icons substituted for the pure and intelligible Idea of God?[12]

Both Father Callahan and Peter Vincent seem to have fallen prey to the "visible machinery of icons" that Baudrillard warns of, losing sight of the "supreme power" those icons represent. Their misplaced faith in the machinery of the icon ironically leads to an actual crisis of faith, one that results in the exodus of the former from the narrative and a cowardly flight from danger for the latter. Callahan, having been forced to drink the blood of Barlow, is last seen in the novel on a bus to anywhere but 'Salem's Lot, later achieving some amount of redemption in Stephen King's *Dark Tower* series. And Peter Vincent flees from the confrontation with the vampire Jerry Dandridge, only to come face-to-face with Evil Ed, now a vampire himself. Vincent also finds a certain level of redemption when he once again faces Dandridge wielding nothing but a cross to protect himself, this time repelling (again, temporarily) the undead fiend. One might wonder how much of this redemption for the Vampire Hunters stems from the power of God represented within the applied machineries of deliverance versus the heroism, courage, and brute force they display within the narrative? Baudrillard continues:

10. Clements, *Vampire Defanged*, 30.

11. Simply translated as a poor substitute.

12. Baudrillard, *Simulacra and Simulation*, 4.

All Western faith and good faith became engaged in this wager on representation: that a sign could refer to the depth of meaning, that a sign could be exchanged for meaning and that something could guarantee this exchange—God of course. But what if God himself can be simulated, that is to say can be reduced to the signs that constitute faith? Then the whole system becomes weightless, it is no longer itself anything but a gigantic simulacrum—not unreal, but a simulacrum, that is to say never exchanged for the real.[13]

In other words, within the traditional vampire narrative, is it the cross of Christ that has come to be associated with the power of God rather than the power of God itself? With regard to the priest who confronts Pinhead with the most sacred of the icons of the church, he finds that they are essentially "weightless," emblems attempting to exchange mere representation of the holy for the profound authenticity of the Divine, reduced to nothing more than knickknacks that attempt to constitute the mystery and authority of the Christian faith.

By the time the crucifix is liquefied by Pinhead or crushed by the hand of Jerry Dandridge or melted by an alluring bride of Dracula, it has descended through the process of what Baudrillard describes as the phases of the image. According to him, the image proceeds through four stages: "[It] is the reflection of profound reality; it masks and denatures a profound reality; it masks the *absence* of a profound reality; it has no relation to any reality whatsoever: it is its own pure simulacrum."[14] The effectiveness of the cross of Christ for Father Callahan and Peter Vincent solely depends on their ability to allow the symbol of their faith to transcend its visible machinery and immerse them in the profound reality that the cross serves as an agent for. As Barlow tells Callahan, it would seem that only faith provides the modicum of power that can be revealed through the various applied machineries of deliverance within the narratives, not the symbols themselves.

The Force Is With Them

In some vampire narratives, the "profound reality" of Baudrillard does not necessarily belong to an easily defined God or religion, and efforts to funnel such immense universal cosmogonic muscle through mass produced ornaments of religious devotion seem to only deaden its effects. In the novel

13. Ibid., 6.
14. Ibid., 6.

Hotel Transylvania, Chelsea Quinn Yarbro writes of the arbitrary nature of the Divine power at play in the vampire narrative:

> There is a Power, which is only that. It is like the rivers, which nurture us and can destroy us. Whether we are prosperous or drowned in floodwaters, the rivers are still the same. So with this Power. And when it lifts us up and opens our eyes to goodness and wonders, so that we are ennobled and inspired to kindness and excellence, we call it God. But when it is used for pain and suffering and degradation, we call it Satan. The Power is both. It is our use alone which makes it one or the other.[15]

This power as defined by Yarbro is neither defined as good, evil, Christian, or Satanic; it just *is*. At the climax of the novel *'Salem's Lot*, we discover that this power may very well have been available to Father Callahan in his confrontation with Barlow if he had not unquestioningly relied only on the *symbol* of that power, as Mark Petrie watches Ben Mears use an axe doused in holy water to rip through a cellar door, behind which resides the reposing place of Barlow:

> A hard sense of sureness clasped him, a feeling of inevitable rightness, of *whiteness* . . . Power, humming up his arms like volts . . . He was a man taken over, possessed, and Mark saw without knowing (or having to know) that the possession was not in the least Christian; the good was more elemental, less refined. It was ore, like something coughed up out of the ground in naked chunks. There was nothing finished about it. It was Force; it was Power; it was whatever moved the greatest wheels of the universe.[16]

As King describes it, the power that Mears taps into in his pursuit of Barlow, while initiated by the blessed vial of holy water, was not inherently Christian in the slightest. Much like the power Yarbro writes of, this power is ineffable, not contained by icons or symbols, perhaps conjured forth as a part of some metaphysical alchemic reaction activated by the rightness of the Vampire Hunters in relation to the wickedness of Barlow.

In some vampire narratives the symbol of the crucifix stands as its own agency of righteousness, neither dependent on the bearer of the icon, the power behind it, nor where it might rest on the spectrum of the phases of the image theorized by Baudrillard. This is most noticeably demonstrated in the films directed by Terence Fisher. Leggett writes, "For Fisher the

15. Yarbro, *Hotel Transylvania*, 62.

16. King, *'Salem's Lot*, 385.

cross can be found virtually anywhere. The cross emerges out of otherwise ordinary elements such as candlesticks and windmills."[17] The ubiquity of the image of the cross in the cinematic world constructed by Fisher[18] inevitably falls into the symbolic deconstruction Baudrillard warned of, where a power and authority is attributed to an icon that has no claim on said power or authority, leading to the cross of Christ losing any and all meaning as a symbol.

This theological problem is on full display in the film *From Dusk Till Dawn* when characters create makeshift crosses with whatever is at their disposal, including a sawed off shotgun, echoing a theme from the Fisher directed *The Horror of Dracula* where Van Helsing uses two candlesticks to temporarily keep the Count at bay and gradually push him into the sunlight. In *From Dusk Till Dawn 2: Texas Blood Money* (1999), the presence of the cruciform is taken to ridiculous heights as the vampires within the film are repelled by the cross-section of the bars of a jail cell door, as well as by the red cross on the back of an ambulance. Similarly, in the Terrence Fisher directed *The Brides of Dracula* (1960), humans are "able to hold Dracula . . . at bay using the cross even though they don't really seem to understand *why* it has this power."[19] In this manner, the cross is transformed into a mindless weapon similar to a firearm, as one does not need to know the machinations or technology behind the gun nor have faith that the gun will work. Influential Christian theologian Paul Tillich writes, "The first and basic characteristic of the symbol is its figurative quality . . . the inner attitude which is oriented to the symbol does not have the symbol itself in view but rather that which is symbolized in it."[20] At this point, Tillich might not take umbrage with the ubiquity of the cross, differing greatly with the view of Baudrillard. From this perspective, a makeshift crucifix, by nature of what Tillich would describe as the characteristic of "innate power" of the symbol, would carry with it some form of power or authority.

In the novel *'Salem's Lot*, Ben Mears and physician Jimmy Cody have decided to sit in the morgue with the corpse of Marjorie Glick when both men realize that they have failed to bring a crucifix. Cody produces two tongue depressors that are taped into the shape of a cross, their

17. Leggett, *Terence Fisher*, 64.

18. This ubiquity is epitomized in Dracula falling under the shadow of a cross cast by a windmill in the 1960 film *The Brides of Dracula*.

19. Leggett, *Terence Fisher*, 73.

20. Tillich, "The Religious Symbol," in *Myth and Symbol*, 15.

voices growing increasingly tense as the sun sets. The duo, neither practicing Christians, bless the impromptu icon by reciting Psalm 23 as the body of Marjorie Glick twitches to life. The freshly risen vampire quickly attacks, and Ben defends himself with the now glowing crucifix, pressing it into her face. King writes:

> Ben's eyes were stunned by a flash of not-light that happened not before his eyes but seemingly behind them. There was the hot and porcine smell of burning flesh. Her scream this time was full-throated and agonized. He sensed rather than saw her throw herself backward . . . She was up again with wolflike agility, her eyes narrowed in pain, yet still filled with her insane hunger. The flesh of her lower jaw was smoking and black. She was snarling at him.[21]

In this account, two flimsy pieces of innocuous wood used for medical and scientific purposes brandished by men with no religious leaning[22] is transformed into a weapon against the undead, reflecting Tillich's idea that the symbol of the crucifix possesses a power distinctive in and of itself. Tillich continues:

> This characteristic is the most important one. It gives to the symbol the reality which it has almost lost in ordinary usage . . . This characteristic is decisive for the distinction between a sign and a symbol. The sign is interchangeable at will. It does not arise from necessity, for it has no inner power. The symbol, however, does possess a necessary character. It cannot be exchanged. It can only disappear when, through dissolution, it loses its inner power . . . In the course of evolution and as a result of the transition from the mystical to the technical view of the world, they have lost their symbolic character, though not entirely. Once having lost their innate power they became signs.[23]

Tillich here could easily be discussing the gradual erasure over the last hundred years of the vampire as a potent theological symbol. However, in the context of the symbolic power of the cross, he seems to be in slack agreement with the phases of the image. Although, while Baudrillard would argue that at the last phase the symbol has no relation whatsoever to the profound reality it once served, Tillich would assert that, no matter how

21. King, *'Salem's Lot*, 303.

22. In this scene played out in the original mini-series *'Salem's Lot* (1979), Ben, before blessing the makeshift cross, mutters, "No atheists in foxholes."

23. Tillich, "The Religious Symbol," 16.

severe the dissolution of the symbol, some power would always remain due to the innate nature of the icon. With regard to the traditional vampire narrative, it might be argued that the vestiges of this "innate power" is what lingers within the applied machineries of deliverance. This avenue of scrutiny is what ultimately leads to the traditional vampire narrative serving as an apologetic for the Christian belief system, as evidenced in the novel *Midnight Mass* where Father Joe attempts to convince his unbelieving niece of the veracity of Christianity:

> He pointed to the gold crucifix hanging from her neck.
>
> "But you wear a cross. Didn't you once tell me you'd die before wearing anything like that?"
>
> "I damn near did die because I *wasn't* wearing one. So now I wear one for perfectly pragmatic reasons. I've never been one for fashion accessories, but if it chases vampires, I want one."
>
> "But you've got to take the next step, Lacey. You've got to ask *why* the undead fear it, *why* it sears their flesh. There's something *there*. When you face that reality, you won't be an atheist or agnostic anymore."[24]

This reality is also evident within the television universe of *Buffy the Vampire Slayer* created by Joss Whedon (an outspoken atheist). In the episode "Never Kill a Boy on the First Date," Buffy's Watcher Giles confronts a vampire with a crucifix. The vampire, pained, asks, "Why does He hurt me?"[25] Perhaps Giles possessed faith in the power behind the crucifix, perhaps the icon possessed an innate power of its own, or perhaps it was something else altogether. With regard to these philosophical and theological exchanges in *Midnight Mass* and *Buffy the Vampire Slayer*, Tillich goes on to address another perspective on the power of symbols, one that creates an interesting wrinkle within the vampire narrative.

It's All In Your Head

In the Roman Polanski directed comedy *The Fearless Vampire Killers*, a young woman wields a crucifix in an attempt to fend off a vampire who was Jewish before his undeath. He smiles and good-naturedly says, "Oy vey, have you got the wrong vampire."[26] This scene gives life to Tillich's

24. Wilson, *Midnight Mass*, 153–154.

25. *Buffy the Vampire Slayer*, "Never Kill a Boy on the First Date," 1997.

26. *The Fearless Vampire Killers*, Polanski, 1967.

belief that a symbol, in order to be effective, must be accepted socially for what it represents.[27] The Jewish community as a whole does not accept the symbolic meaning of the Christian cross of Christ, therefore, according to Tillich, it would not serve as a legitimate source of power for a Jewish person. He writes:

> This implies that the symbol is socially rooted and socially supported. Hence it is not correct to say that a thing is first a symbol and then gains acceptance; the process of becoming a symbol and the acceptance of a symbol belong together. The act by which a symbol is created is a social act[.][28]

Tillich here raises an interesting question within the traditional vampire narrative found in popular culture: What if the power and authority of the crucifix does not lie within the symbol or even within the alleged influence behind it? What if the power of the cross is a residual psychosomatic response of the *vampire*, conditioned by his or her own religious, cultural, and social norms at work within their psychological development? In the novel *I Am Legend* by Richard Matheson, Robert Neville, the protagonist and survivor of a worldwide viral pandemic that has turned most of the planet into vampires, is explaining to Ruth, another apparent survivor, what he has discovered about the creatures:

> "When I showed him the cross," he said, "he laughed in my face."
> She nodded once.
> "But when I held a torah before his eyes, I got the reaction I wanted."
> "A what?"
> "A torah. Tablet of law, I believe it is."
> "And that . . . got a reaction?"
> "Yes, I had him tied up, but when he saw the torah he broke loose and attacked me . . . So you see, the cross hasn't the power the legend says it has. My theory is that, since the legend came into its own in Europe, a continent predominantly Catholic, the cross would naturally become the symbol of defense against powers of darkness."[29]

---

27. This raises the question of why God will not (or is unable to) imbue the Christian symbol with power outright, aside from whether said symbol is accepted in a social setting or not.

28. Tillich, *Religious Symbol*, 16.

29. Matheson, *I Am Legend*, 129.

Similarly, in *Dracula 2000*, this concept of the vampire as its own moral and ethical agency is explored further, albeit as a punch line, when vampire Marcus (Omar Epps) attacks Simon (Jonny Lee Miller), a reluctant Vampire Hunter, who brandishes a cross while defending himself from the creature. Marcus grins widely and says, "Sorry sport, I'm an atheist."[30]

Continuing this post-modern theme, in the first book of the popular *Twilight* series, the vampire Edward, during a tour of his home, shows Bella a large wooden Christian cross hanging in an upstairs hallway. While Bella is somewhat surprised by this, a conversation regarding the history of the carved work of art comes across as somewhat mundane and provides no indication of any adverse effects on the vampire beside her.

In addition, Matheson, through Neville, expands further on this concept when he writes, "'Why should a Jew fear the cross? Why should a vampire who had been a Jew fear it? Most people were afraid of becoming vampires. But as far as the cross goes — well, neither a Jew nor a Hindu nor a Mohammedan nor an atheist, for that matter, would fear the cross.'"[31] These narrative examples build upon earlier questions in this book as to the ambivalence of God toward evil. Why would the omnipotent Divine not lend unlimited power to the warriors representing the sacred order of the cosmos? Why was the serpent given license to influence the actions of Adam and Eve? Or even created in the first place? And how does the righteousness of God not supersede the sway and power of evil in the world?

Interreligious Horror

While this psychological explanation has undoubtedly contributed to the secularization of the traditional vampire narrative that Susannah Clements mourns, removing the religious symbolism, metaphors, and analogies for a more pseudoscientific and psychologically based explanation of the undead might actually provide an opportunity for a discussion of religious pluralism in a post-modern society. If the traditional vampire narrative and its associated symbolism within popular culture is losing influence (along with the lessening influence of religion in society overall), perhaps the vampire might find new life as the catalyst for fresh dialogue on what needs to transpire for religion to maintain relevance within society. In order to remain germane to a far more savvy and enlightened audience than what existed when Count

30. Lussier, 2000.
31. Matheson, *I Am Legend*, 123.

Dracula first journeyed to England in 1897, the figure of the vampire needs to evolve beyond merely a symbol of Christian exceptionalism.

In her book *A Feminist Ethic of Risk*, Sharon Welch writes, "[T]he triumph of evil in much of history makes untenable the claims of classic theism. The basic question of theodicy — Given the existence of so much evil in the world, how can God be both loving and all-powerful? — is not a new one. In examining this problem I concur with those who find that the existence of evil falsifies the claim of omnipotence."[32] Similar to the religious equalization we see occur in Matheson's novel *I Am Legend* where all sacred ideologies seem to bear some amount of secularization, perhaps an effective route to utilizing a transcendent belief system would be to remove God from the equation altogether. In this sense, removing the Divine as a figure with independent agency would not so much constitute *eliminating* the transcendent aspect of religion but *deemphasizing* what some might perceive as the immutable and unchanging precepts, laws, and declarations of a particular deity or Divine force, essentially discarding the immanence of God. Welch argues that we should be "referring to divinity, not as a noun or even a verb, but as an adjective or adverb. Divinity then connotes a quality of relationships, lives, events, and natural processes that are worthy of worship, that provide orientation, focus, and guidance to our lives."[33] Welch's theological reframing does not necessarily remove the Divine from religion; it places the onus of spiritual growth and development on the wider community, not upon inscrutable scriptures viewed as the moral precepts of an ancient sky idol. The narratives and ethics that emerge from these scriptures are then viewed through the lens of a particular community, allowing for the freedom of a diversity of interpretations versus a society rigidly defined by those ethics, which can often lead to intransigence emerging out of the perceived exceptionalism of a particular religious view. In essence, it is a matter of emphasizing a theology of transcendence and deemphasizing one of immanence.

To a large extent, this book thus far has been an effort to view the vampire less as a distinctive apologetic for the supremacy of Christianity and more as a complex reflection on the enmeshment of God and evil. Thusly, the goal has not been to disavow anyone of the benefits of religion as a positive meaning system. Rather, it has been designed to rescue the vampire from those who interpret religion as a form of ethical and moral agency,

32. Welch, *A Feminist Ethic of Risk*, 175.
33. Ibid., 176.

hijacking and twisting Scripture, using it as the basis for moral judgment and ethical agency. However, what if the immutable status of Scripture was deemphasized, placing prominence on communal standards influencing scriptural interpretation? If religious precepts and ethics are considered sacred then they consequently must originate from the will of the Divine, existing as the only true or right precepts and ethics by which one can live life. However, when interpretive strategies are utilized that focus on the betterment of the community, it makes sense for those strategies be directed toward solving or alleviating tangible problems at play in society, with sacred rituals and moral proclamations deemphasized for the sake of cooperation, growth, and spiritual health.

These strategies would also swing wide the gate to a plurality of religious perspectives and interactions. Interreligious relations, while a broad category in general, tend to imply a vision of constructive and peaceful work between differing faith traditions. And while this is undoubtedly an integral component of interreligious relations, it must also be acknowledged that, despite the generalized message of peace at the core of most major religious traditions, very real tensions exist amidst these various groups, anxieties that can sometimes manifest through conflict and violence. This is made possible, in part, by the ethical ambivalence of religion and its scriptures.

With an acknowledgement of the potential for positive social and cultural impact religion contains within itself, the work of interreligious relations might not only provide an engine by which multidisciplinary work can be enacted to further peaceful interactions within diverse religious traditions, it also holds the potential to serve as a tool by which differing traditions might learn more about their own religious values and traditions.

Unfortunately, the broad model of interreligious relations is an impossibly large mechanism with innumerable moving parts, often facing ideological and theological roadblocks toward effective dialogue that must be carefully traversed in order to reach any type of working arrangement. One of these moving parts is the general concern over syncretism, or the blending of two distinct religious faiths, an interreligious bugaboo fraught with fear and anxiety. The firewall of syncretism succeeds in constructing barriers of division between the faithful from varied religious journeys. Ultimately, we must question what the underlying fear of interreligious dialogue really is. With regard to Christianity, are scriptural narratives so delicate as to require human agency to protect them from some of type impure religious miscegenation? Is the Christian God not powerful enough to prevent syncretism?[34] Differing religious faiths can toil side-by-side and arm-in-arm without losing the distinguishing uniqueness each tradition brings to their body of faith. There is plenty of religious space for differing faith communities to work together (and possibly even enmesh where traditions provide overlap) toward the mutual goal of social betterment.

As faith systems cooperate in order to advance the cause of interreligious movements, it is the intentional act of acknowledging differences that creates an atmosphere of mutual appreciation of our shared, yet distinct, spiritual journeys. In order to celebrate and labor together, notions of religious exceptionalism need to be set aside, trusting that unique faiths will not ultimately be corrupted by the presence of an incompatible belief system. Religious adherents should possess confidence in the strength of their personal and corporate convictions superseding any efforts (indirect or otherwise) at syncretism.

Forging cooperative solutions through the rich diversity of religious dogmas would provide a plethora of narratives for social justice and cultural transformation. Religion is able to provide meaning from both an analogous and metaphorical standpoint, with the presence of the Divine incidental to the narratives that bond a community in shared meaning. Religion with the Divine deemphasized actually calls for a deeper reading of Scripture, focusing less on a strictly documentary interpretation of the passages ("God said it, that settles it") while encouraging the interpreter to pay closer attention to hermeneutic process. By engaging in the analytical exercises of critical history, literary critique, and historicism, a rich spiritual narrative emerges. This model of interpreting scripture (one we will explore further in the following chapter) works contrary to viewing passages in the light of Christological and salvific doctrines, eschewing relatively modern theological cipher disks of literalism that are counterproductive as models of interpretation, whether with regard to contemporary ethics, theology, or even the purpose of the vampire narrative in popular culture.

---

34. The history and development of Christianity is littered with examples of syncretism, as the emergent religion commandeered the sacred components of the diverse cultures it sought to usurp.

5

Vamp Check! Vamp Check!: The Vampire Narrative as Model of Social Change

"Humans need to tell stories. It's a fundamental and uniting thing. It's through stories that we come to understand ourselves and we come to understand the world."

–KEVIN (TOM HOLLANDER) FROM BYZANTIUM[1]

THERE IS SOME SENSE of irony in framing the vampire narrative as a catalyst for positive social change. Most noticeably, Dracula and his breed are, more often than not, sinister characters, admittedly devoid of love[2] and seeking only self-gratification, mirrored in any number of literary and cinematic creations such as Count Orlok in the silent film *Nosferatu* (1922), Barlow in *Salem's Lot*, or Santanico Pandemonium in the movie *From Dusk Till Dawn*. Most vampires in traditional narratives follow suit, with occasional sympathetic, yet fleeting, glimpses into their plight. For example, the vampire Jerry Dandridge in *Fright Night* attacks protagonist Charley Brewster, telling him, "You deserve to die, boy. Of course, I can give you something I don't have. A choice."[3] While it might give one pause to hear that a vampire such as Dandridge was turned against his will, it doesn't change the fact

---

1. *Byzantium*, Jordan, 2013.

2. Notwithstanding the romantic re-envisioning of Dan Curtis and Francis Ford Coppola's respective takes on the figure of Dracula.

3. Holland, 1985.

that he is fully embracing his current role as an active agent of oppression. Contrastingly, in the novel *Midnight Mass*, a post-human Father Joe, rather than perpetuate or take part in the system of vampiric oppression he is now a part of, uses his "privilege" as a member of the dominant vampire class to affect change, ultimately destroying the undead power structure.

This figure of the revolutionary vampire is echoed in characters such as the half-human/half-vampire Marvel superhero Blade,[4] Angelus from the *Buffy the Vampire Slayer* universe, and Henry Sturges and his sympathetic vampire brethren who, in Seth Grahame-Smith's novel *Abraham Lincoln: Vampire Hunter*, stand and fight with the sixteenth President of the United States against the tyrannical population of vampires who have enmeshed themselves into the American slave trade. However, in the case of Jerry Dandridge lamenting his lack of choice with regard to being a vampire, Susannah Clements would argue that he always had an option to resist his vampiric urges, and that to submit to the dark power of the vampire was to give in to sin. As previously discussed in *Such a Dark Thing*, Clements uses Bram Stoker's *Dracula* to argue that the vampire stands in direct opposition to the Divine, an anti-Christ representing all that is unholy and debauched within God's created order. Thusly, a truly righteous man would oppose such a fate at all costs.

The view of Clements as to the power and allure of the vampire is, in some ways, reflected in the vampires that inhabit both the town and novel *'Salem's Lot*, a book which Stephen King has publicly stated is a form of literary homage to Bram Stoker's *Dracula*. In the following passage from *'Salem's Lot*, Danny Glick, a recent vampire convert, visits young Mark Petrie in the middle of the night. Danny floats ominously outside of the window of the bedroom, forebodingly scratching at the glass until Mark wakes up and fully grasps the awfulness before him:

> [Mark] got out of bed and almost fell down. It was only then that he realized fright was too mild a word for this. Even terror did not express what he felt. The pallid face outside the window tried to smile, but it had lain in darkness too long to remember precisely how. What Mark saw was a twitching grimace – a bloody mask of tragedy ... "Mark, let me in! I command it! *He* commands it!"
>
> He was weakening. That whispering voice was seeing through his barricade, and the command was imperative. Mark's eyes fell

4. Blade first appeared in 1973 in issue #10 of Marvel's *Tomb of Dracula* comic book series.

on his desk, littered with his model monsters, now so bland and foolish —

His eyes fixed abruptly on part of the display, and widened slightly.

The plastic ghoul was walking through a plastic graveyard and one of the monuments was in the shape of a cross . . . Mark swept up the cross, curled it into a tight fist, and said loudly: "come on in, then."

The face became suffused with an expression of vulpine triumph. The window slid up and Danny stepped in and took two paces forward . . . The head cocked, doglike, the upper lip curled away from those shining canines.

Mark brought the plastic cross around in a vicious swipe and laid it against Danny Glick's cheek.[5]

On the surface, this passage seems to augment the notion that vampires metaphorically represent temptation and sin, with the only avenue for resistance lying within the power of the cross of Christ, prompting Douglas Winter, in his book *Stephen King: The Art of Darkness,* to observe that the vampires in the novel 'Salem's Lot contain "important metaphors for the seductiveness of evil and the dehumanizing pall of modern society."[6] However, with regard to the above passage, what had Mark done to place himself in such dire straits? If, for whatever reason, he were unable to snatch the plastic cross from his model, would he have been doomed to roam the darkened streets of the Lot as a member of the undead, scratching on the windows of unsuspecting victims?

In his non-fiction work *Danse Macabre,* Stephen King touches on this issue when he discusses the novel *Dracula.* "Harker's ordeal at Castle Dracula is not the result of an inner sin or weakness; he winds up on the Count's doorstep because his boss asked him to go."[7] And it is here where we begin to dissect the commonly held view that the traditional vampire narrative within the popular culture is a Christian parable, a *direct* religious allegory for sin.

---

5. King, 'Salem's Lot, 231–232.

6. Winter, Stephen King: The Art of Darkness, 37.

7. King, Danse Macabre, 66.

A Symbol of Resistance and Liberation

While any serious conversation about the western vampire narrative within popular culture is undoubtedly a theological one, it cannot be overstated that victims of the undead are often undeserving of their fate, ultimately enslaved by a power far greater and more oppressive than any individual can address. Within Bram Stoker's *Dracula*, neither Jonathan Harker, Lucy Westenra, or Mina Harker display any type of moral or ethical failure that deservedly brought about the (un)natural consequence of the vampire. Therefore, it would seem that the theological implications of the traditional vampire narrative as it pertains to the concept of sin hinge less on the previously discussed Augustinian model and more on a liberationist critique of theology and ethics, one where the vampire comes to represent a communal sin such as poverty or institutionalized racism versus individual moral failings.

Originating amongst the Catholic priests and clergy of Latin America in the 1950s, liberation theology has developed as something of a rebellious branch of Christian thought and philosophy. Centered on tearing down unjust social and economic structures, liberation theology "attempts to reflect on the experience and meaning of the Christian faith based on the commitment to abolish injustice and to build a new society."[8] This form of theological thought filters scriptural precepts through the eyes of the oppressed in society, focusing more on providing freedom from institutionalized evil versus a theology of individualized and personal salvation.[9]

While liberation theology appears to reflect the mandate for social change espoused by Jesus within the Gospels, it is often attacked and maligned for its connection to Marxist ideologies and progressive views of society and social justice, particularly the ongoing critique of capitalism espoused by liberationist theologians. This specific theological perspective is so threatening to some that it is often used to disparage individuals and groups wholesale, as demonstrated by conservative radio personality Glenn Beck accusing President Barack Obama in 2010 of adhering to the tenets of liberation theology and proclaiming, "That is not a Christian belief."[10]

8. Gutiérrez, "A Theology of Liberation," in *Readings in Christian Ethics*, 345.

9. Corporate sin and personal sin are not necessarily mutually exclusive. However, liberation theology is less concerned with the popular evangelical notion of accepting Jesus as a personal lord and savior and more focused on the idea of comprehensive social transformation.

10. "Glenn Beck Sticks 'Liberation Theology' Label on Obama's Christianity," *The Christian Science Monitor*, August 25, 2010.

A month later, Beck dedicated his entire radio show to attacking libera-tion theology,[11] the concept of social justice,[12] and specifically condemning black liberation theologian James Cone. Similarly, conservative voices have been outraged by the overt stance Pope Francis has taken against unchecked capitalism and wealth, as well as his seeming reversal of the longstanding Catholic censure against liberation theology.[13]

Whether one considers liberation theology controversial, heretical, or culturally indispensable, it is germane with regard to the traditional vam-pire narrative and the religious motifs therein. Oppression and freedom are common themes within these stories as the vampire quite comfortably fits into the role of institutionalized and entrenched power, making the lens of liberation theology through which to view the vampire narrative a perti-nent one. We see this epitomized in Barlow gradually enslaving an entire town in the novel 'Salem's Lot, while in Midnight Mass the vampiric revolu-tion strikes quickly and overtly, dominating most of civilized society. In the David Sosnowski penned Vamped, as well as the film Daybreakers (2009), vampire dominion and oppression is so entirely comprehensive that hu-manity has become nothing more than chattel, existing in factories where they are regularly processed for blood supplies. Similarly, in the recent New York Times bestselling The Strain trilogy of novels written by Chuck Hogan and Guillermo del Toro, vampires enslave and oppress humanity by sabo-taging nuclear reactors, resulting in an atomic winter that generates a literal permanent midnight around the world.

In this sense, the societal oppression demonstrated within the tradi-tional vampire narrative could easily serve as a shockingly apt metaphor for Latin American, Black, Womanist, Feminist, or even Queer Liberation Theologies, any movement that develops as a response to the subjugation (physical, spiritual, or emotional) of an entire group of people, up to and including the recent Occupy Wall Street movement.[14]

11. "Glenn Beck Takes on Liberation Theology," Religion Dispatches, July 19, 2010.

12. Earlier that same year, Beck infamously told his radio audience, "I beg you, look for the words 'social justice' or 'economic justice' on your church web site. If you find it, run as fast as you can. Social justice and economic justice, they are code words. Now, am I advising people to leave their church? Yes! If you have a priest that is pushing social justice, go find another parish." Christianity Today.

13. Soon after Bishop Jorge Mario Bergoglio became Pope Francis, he invited Gustavo Gutiérrez, whose writings are quoted in this book, to the Vatican for Mass and breakfast.

14. The metaphor of vampire-as-corporate-oppressor is so culturally apt that a popu-lar piece of artwork from famed artist Alex Ross depicting former POTUS George W.

The emergence of Occupy Wall Street in September 2011 rapidly transformed into a significant popular social uprising, inspired, in some respect, by the culture altering revolutions witnessed in the events surrounding the Arab Spring less than a year earlier. Despite being forced out of Zuccotti Park in New York City and other locations around the country, Occupy Wall Street has proven pliable enough to mature outside of its infancy born within the power of protest and has come to serve as a catalyst for modern civilization to examine the ubiquity of inequality and financial tyranny throughout society. Occupy Wall Street operated as a modern day biblical prophet crying out against the corruption and greed surrounding the capitalistic fervor and indomitable corporatism that subjugates millions of people around the globe. In this sense, the Occupy Wall Street revolution and its current incarnations such as the Rolling Jubilee and Strike Debt movements not only bear the undeniable marks of liberationist ethics, it also becomes a relevant contemporary model by which we can examine the vampire narrative and how it still maintains relevant symbolic life in a post-religious society.

Timothy Beal, while discussing the novel *Dracula*, illustrates the potential reach and power of the vampire as a dominant social and cultural oppressor when he writes, "Dracula's arrival in England represents a crisis of apocalyptic proportions. His invasion threatens not only the individual bodies and souls of those who come in contact with him . . . but the entire cosmos. Dracula threatens to contaminate the sacred purity of all of creation, from body to house to nation to cosmos."[15] Such an all-encompassing and destructive invasion moves beyond privatized sin into a corporate and shared spiritual oppression with immediate and eternal consequences. The prevailing cultural and corporate vampires Occupy Wall Street stood against pose a similar threat to society, corrupting everything from the electoral process, to education, to affordable health care, to how our news is collected and disseminated amidst an atmosphere of corporate influence and profit margins. Chris Hedges, in his New York Times bestselling book *Days of Destruction Days of Revolt*, writes, "The elites have exposed their hand. They have shown they have nothing to offer. They can destroy but they cannot build. They can repress but they cannot lead. They can steal

---

Bush as a vampire, sinking his fangs into the Statue of Liberty, an answer to the pro-corporate policies of said administration, went viral on the Internet.

15. Beal, *Religion and Its Monsters*, 129.

but they cannot share."[16] In other words, these powerful financial incubi are dead; dead in spirit, dead to compassion, and dead to love. And they seek to control and consume all that exists within their corrupt vision and insatiable hunger.

Seen through this lens, the vampire narrative might then serve as a form of what ethicist Sharon Welch describes as resistance literature, works that have developed out of marginalized communities over the last century that convey an ongoing struggle for liberation. She writes, "The function of telling particular stories of oppression and resistance is not to find the 'one true story' of subjugation and revolt but is to elicit other stories of suffering and courage, of defeat, of tragedy and resilient creativity."[17] And while Welch, who used Womanist writings such as Paule Marshall's *The Chosen Place, The Timeless People*, Toni Morrison's *The Bluest Eye*, and Toni Cade Bambara's *The Salt-Eaters* as her examples, might scoff at the idea of the traditional vampire narrative serving as a form of resistance literature, it is difficult not to see strains of this resistance within the movements of the intrepid, though outmatched, Vampire Hunters who emerge audaciously out of a subjugated culture to stand against the seeming unconquerable vampire. Welch goes on to state, "The collective telling of stories is the foundation for seeing and then challenging patterns of systematic injustice,"[18] a pattern that repeats itself throughout the history of the vampire narrative in popular culture.

In response to systematic injustice, liberation theology embeds its ideology within the distress and subjugation of peoples and cultures that have been marginalized, abused, starved out, and forgotten, with an eschatological perspective that seeks to transform the very structure of society and reversing or eradicating the oppressive invasion of whatever dominant hierarchy exists. In his essay "A Theology of Liberation," Gustavo Gutiérrez explains that "the present in the praxis of liberation, in its deepest dimension, is pregnant with the future" and that "it means sinking roots where the pulse of history is beating at this moment."[19] Whether serving to free Mina Harker in *Dracula*, Amy in *Fright Night*, the town of Jerusalem's Lot, or the entire human race in *Midnight Mass*, the activists serving as the catalyst for freedom embodies the praxis of liberation, serving deeply and fully in the

16. Hedges and Sacco, *Days of Destruction, Days of Revolt*, 232.

17. Welch, *Feminist Ethic of Risk*, 139.

18. Ibid., 128.

19. Gutiérrez, "Theology of Liberation," 343.

present with a confidence of a liberated future. Welch adds, "The present is described not so much as a series of inevitable facts but as the impetus for defiance and transformation."[20] This sureness of the impending outcome of events is neither flippant nor boastful. Rather, it is shaped and informed by the struggle thus far, by those who have unfortunately succumbed, and by the knowledge that those currently resisting may also be asked to pay the ultimate price to secure spiritual, emotional, and physical liberation.

In addition, liberation theology involves confrontation, as it deals with challenging the systems of the oppressor and the oppressed. In most vampire narratives the climax often involves a grand confrontation between the Vampire Hunters and the dominant vampiric agent of oppression. This clash, while generally violent in nature, does potentially reveal an important symbolic nuance with regard to a liberationist critique of the traditional vampire narrative. James Cone, in his essay "A Black Theology of Liberation," writes, "In the New Testament, Jesus is not for all, but for the oppressed, the poor and unwanted of society, and against oppressors. The God of the biblical tradition is not uninvolved or neutral regarding human affairs; rather he is quite involved. He is active in human history, taking sides with the oppressed of the land."[21] Cone goes on to state that it is impossible for God to be on the side of both the oppressed and the oppressor, like a glorified cosmic referee desperate to maintain some conciliation among humanity. Approaching the traditional vampire narrative through this lens opens a new perspective on why the various icons and applied machineries of deliverance have some effect when used in the course of doing battle with the vampire. And while we must still ask why God does not simply show up and crush the tyrannical nature of the vampire, this partiality could be seen as a positive indicator of Divine preference for the oppressed.

Finally, there is the need for solidarity among practitioners of liberation theology. Described by feminist theologian Ada Maria Isasi-Diaz as "understanding the interconnections among issues and the cohesiveness that needs to exist among the communities of struggle,"[22] solidarity is less about agreement and more about shared feelings concerning the state of the oppressed in our world. She writes, "Solidarity with the oppressed and among the oppressed has to be at the heart of Christian behavior, because

20. Welch, *Feminist Ethic of Risk*, 141.

21. Cone, "A Black Theology of Liberation," *Readings in Christian Ethics: A Historical Sourcebook*, 360.

22. Isasi-Diaz, "Love of Neighbor in the 1980s," *Feminist Theological Ethics*, 78–79.

the oppression suffered by the majority affects everyone."[23] Throughout the traditional vampire narrative within popular culture, a common thread is the struggle of the solitary believer to persuade potential allies that vampires threaten to contaminate "the sacred purity of all of creation." While Ben Mears in 'Salem's Lot was undoubtedly convinced of this danger, the empirically thoughtful Dr. Cody needed some persuading before running around town pounding stakes into the chests of friends and neighbors. He was, however, willing to provide Mears the creative space required to convince the physician that the horror of vampiric oppression was a legitimate menace. Welch writes, "The intention of solidarity is potentially more inclusive and more transformative than is the goal of consensus," and that an element of solidarity involves "granting each group sufficient respect to listen to their ideas and to be challenged by them."[24] While it was not required of Cody to believe the improbable story shared by Mears in order to stand in solidarity with him, it *was* necessary to understand that the two were "so intertwined that each is accountable to the other,"[25] thus necessitating an environment and atmosphere of receptiveness to the oppression one perceives and/or is experiencing in the world.

In the vampire narrative, solidarity is achieved through the formation of individuals into a community whereby they not only identify with the victim of the vampire, they take active steps to address and ameliorate said oppression. In the novel *Dracula*, Jonathan Harker is moved into action after being subject to the domination of the Count, while Dr. Seward, Quincey Morris and Arthur Holmwood respond to the spiritual and physical subjugation of the undead after encountering Lucy Westenra in her vampiric state. In 'Salem's Lot, solidarity is crucial to any movement against the dark oppression Barlow inflicts on the town, and individual acts of heroism are muted next to unified cohesive strategies. Edward Ingebretsen addresses this in his book *Maps of Heaven, Maps of Hell: Religious Terror as Memory from the Puritans to Stephen King*:

> 'Salem's Lot reflects a low-Protestant vision of theological democracy in which the individual stands alone in moral combat against unseen forces. Any power that will be displayed is organized communally; the secret revelation is dis-covered by concerted effort as

23. Ibid., 80.
24. Welch, *Feminist Ethic of Risk*, 132–133.
25. Ibid., 133.

Ben and Mark gradually establish a relationship of mutual love by means of which they defeat the enemy.[26]

Matt Burke, Ben Mears, Mark Petrie, Susan Norton, Dr. Cody, and Father Callahan form a community of faith and action that fails when solidarity is fractured, represented in the separation of the group both physically and ideologically, agents working individually versus together as a stronger singular entity. Susan, Cody, and Callahan are all easily dispatched due to their eagerness to operate outside of the solidarity of the community, reflecting the view of Welch that "Despair is avoided by an embrace of community."[27] Ben and Mark seem to understand this, only surviving as a result of the bond forged between them due to the oppression that has befallen the town and the rest of their team.

An Agent of Liberation?

In his book *Journey to the Common Good*, theologian Walter Brueggemann embarks on a detailed examination of the narrative of the Jewish exodus out of Egypt, discussing ways it can serve as a model for how modern society might work toward a comprehensive common good and away from structures of political, economic, military and ideological oppression. Even though the Hebrew Scriptures are "permeated with impediments to the common good, including the pervasive influence of patriarchy, ethnicity, race, sect, and party, not even to mention the layers of human and Divine anger that pervade its pages,"[28] Brueggemann believes that a type of *double read* of the ancient text can provide modern culture with a roadmap out of the "defining nature of the empire of force among us."[29] This double read of the Exodus narrative is pertinent as we conduct a similar exercise with respect to the traditional western vampire narrative in popular culture, particularly as it pertains to the idea of the revolt metaphor put forth in this chapter.

While Brueggemann primarily focuses on the configuration of empire through a militaristic lens, he does write, "Slavery in the Old Testament happens because the strong ones work a monopoly over the weak ones, and eventually exercise control over their bodies. Not only that; in

26. Ingenbretsen, *Maps of Heaven, Maps of Hell,* 179.

27. Welch, *Feminist Ethic of Risk,* 144.

28. Brueggemann, *Journey to the Common Good,* 1.

29. Ibid., 115.

the end the peasants, now become slaves, are grateful for their dependent status."[30] Working from this portrayal, the concept of empire for Brueggemann exists within any system that emphasizes restless productivity and consumption over the unique agency of the population within that system.

In response to such a structure of subjugation, Brueggemann argues for a reaction of in-depth theological study and "an exercise in the art of departure, an enterprise that focuses upon the great traditions of critical reflection that are resources for thinking outside the box, for making decisions to be agents in our own history and not chattel for a system of production and consumption."[31] For Brueggemann, the work of departure involves the intentional dreaming and acting "outside imperial reality. And dreaming outside imperial reality, that human agents can begin the daring extrication of this people from the imperial system."[32]

This condition of subjugation and the act of departure is clearly evident in the novel 'Salem's Lot where the vampiric overthrow of Jerusalem's Lot was only made possible by the utter lack of communal solidarity within the town *before* the arrival of Barlow. This is best illustrated by Parkins Gillespie, the town constable: "'It ain't alive,' Parkins said, lighting his smoke with a wooden kitchen match. 'That's why he came here. It's dead, like him. Has been for twenty years or more.'"[33] The town, fractured and paranoid, and perhaps still mourning their complicity in the legacy of the vile and depraved Hubert Marsten, a dark and unabashedly evil figure in the history of the Lot, is filled with the very real horrors of child abuse, intimate partner violence, predatory financial schemes, alcoholism, and murder, all shielded from view by a protective membranous skin of emotional and spiritual malaise blanketing the inhabitants.

The manner in which Stephen King renders these everyday horrors within his fictional town is of particular importance to the novel, and to the relation of the traditional vampire narrative serving as a form of resistance literature and liberative communication. Terror and dread emanating from the familiar and everyday, whether the bucolic small town of 'Salem's Lot, a suburb of New Jersey in *Midnight Mass*, a peaceful all-American neighborhood in *Fright Night*, Victorian era England in *Dracula*, or even the bustling and insomnious world of Manhattan as portrayed in *The Strain*

30. Ibid., 6.
31. Ibid., 31.
32. Ibid., 12.
33. King, 'Salem's Lot, 378.

series of books, is far more disturbing and menacing than any dystopian futures. King provides a lens into the often mundane and hidden revulsion of small town life, a credible palette from which the otherworldly terror of the vampire ultimately invades. Welch writes, "[C]ontemporary communities are flawed — unable to see as unjust the inequality crucial to it its functioning."[34] A vampire narrative such as 'Salem's Lot highlights the injustices of contemporary life, serving as a metaphorical lens by which we might examine the struggles of inequality that are knowingly obfuscated by the larger community.

Hallab addresses how King "rather unsympathetically shows what can happen to the people in a small town who have lost their sense of community and their faith . . . The failure of religion to inspire true faith — in their God, in their fellow beings, or even in themselves[.]"[35] From this perspective, one could even view the master vampire Barlow as an agent of liberation in Salem's Lot, an undead Moses delivering a welcome reprieve or salvation to a people who have long lived under an invisible (and perhaps self-inflicted) yoke of oppression. In her article entitled "Women and Vampires: Nightmare or Utopia?" Judith Johnson writes:

> King carefully creates, one by one, the ordinarily human, selfish, and stupid inhabitants of his Maine town . . . When the vampire strikes, and begins to victimize the town, some of these natural predators become victims, thus receiving a kind of justice . . . [T]he born victims . . . now become vampires . . . By the end of the novel, the whole town has risen in a kind of parodic revolution and become a vampire town, a town of the revolting, in all sense of the word, a town that won't allow itself to be abused.[36]

This revolt metaphor in 'Salem's Lot, hearkening back to a similar theme within the Exodus narrative and Welch's resistance literature, finds camaraderie with many vampire mythologies both traditional and contemporary. In Fright Night, Jerry Dandridge offers Evil Ed freedom from his bullying and the opportunity to no longer play victim to his teenage oppressors. In the HBO series True Blood, based on the Sookie Stackhouse novels by Charlaine Harris, the vampires can be seen to serve as a stand-in for the LGBTQI community, refusing any longer to accept second-class citizenry from the dominant heterosexual culture. Even in the distinctly

34. Welch, Feminist Ethic of Risk, 125.

35. Hallab, Vampire God, 100.

36. Johnson, "Women and Vampires: Nightmare or Utopia?" 72–80.

non-religious universe of the *Blade* film series, the vampire is presented as the next level of existence, achieving freedom from the oppression, triviality, and frailty inherent in the human condition.

Of course, the theory of the vampire serving as an agent of liberation certainly has its share of flaws. In the case of *'Salem's Lot*, as well as most other vampire narratives, a vampire, once turned, must create more victims in order to sustain itself. As Johnson points out, previously living oppressors and victims alike are now predators in their new role as vampire. "In their turn, they act out their predatory nature, victimizing others as they used to do when they were alive. But these others, the born victims, victimized again by the predators, now become vampires. *They, too, find someone upon whom to prey*" (italics added).[37] A theology or ethic of liberation seeks a radical break from the *status quo* versus propping up the prevailing cultural hegemony at work in a society that makes, knowing or otherwise, conspirators of the oppressed with regard to maintaining the dominant power structure.

While it might be difficult to imagine that a community would not realize it is being oppressed or even be complicit in their own oppression, we see this dynamic take place every election cycle within the United States when millions of Americans actively vote against their social and financial interests. From women voting for a Republican party that attempted unsuccessfully to block the 2013 reauthorization of the Violence Against Women Act and managed to successfully block the 2014 Paycheck Fairness Act, to individuals from an array of social and economic strata electing politicos who provide tax breaks for the wealthiest among us while consistently shrinking the social safety net desperately needed by the poorest of society,[38] Welch was prescient in her observation that contemporary communities are "unable to see as unjust the inequality" seemingly dyed into the wool of prevailing American society.

With regard to the vampire serving as an agent of deliverance, it is imperative to note that liberation theology is never about replacing one form of dominance for another, arguably modeled in the continual pendulous cycle of futile electorate reciprocation we experience within the United States that does little more than exchange one political party for another, an

37. Johnson, "Women and Vampires," 77.

38. Not just a consequence of conservative politics, Democratic President Barak Obama supported and signed the 2014 Farm Bill, legislation that provided billions of dollars to corporate agricultural interests while cutting nearly $9 billion from Supplemental Nutrition Assistance Program (SNAP) benefits over a ten-year period.

outmoded ritual that grows increasingly repressive and degrading as disturbingly unlimited amounts of corporate money pour into the American political process, effectively placing 300 million citizens at the mercy of a capricious and ravenous monster that only responds to its wealthy and oppressive masters. This does more to exacerbate the problem of authoritative hierarchical structures than actually eliminate them. Rather, liberation theology and ethics seek to erase the dynamic of domination and coercion altogether. In most vampire narratives, living hierarchical structures are only exchanged for undead ones, whether it be the authority Dracula has over his brides and the nearby villagers, the undemocratic power structure of the vampire community in *True Blood*,[39] or references to Barlow as the "Master" in *'Salem's Lot*.[40]

This returns the discussion to the absolute need for solidarity within a community to combat oppression. It should be noted, however, contrary to the insights expressed by Ingebretsen, that solidarity is not a guarantee of success. A unified Ben Mears and Mark Petrie fail to overcome the enemy in *'Salem's Lot*, an important observation when exploring the vampire narrative and liberation theology. In fact, despite Barlow being destroyed, the town of 'Salem's Lot never quite emerges from its oppression, and vampires still roam the countryside as evidenced in the short-story sequel penned by King entitled *One For the Road*. The story, set several years after the events of the novel, is centered on two men from a neighboring town who must brave their unspoken fears in order to help a family stranded by a snowstorm in the ghostly remains of Jerusalem's Lot.

This is not to argue that the efforts of the Vampire Hunters are futile. Welch writes, "The fact that we experience moments of defeat, of being outmaneuvered, does not mean that the power in our movements for justice is not divine."[41] In the ongoing struggle for liberation, perfect or even adequate endings are never guaranteed as history has continuously revealed the tragedy and misfortune of countless marginalized and oppressed communities. In his book *A Theology of Liberation: History, Politics, and Salvation*, Gustavo Gutiérrez argues that the work against oppression is long,

---

39. Kings and queens rule various territories within the *True Blood* universe.

40. In *The Dark Tower: Wolves of the Calla*, Stephen King fleshes this power structure out when Barlow is revealed to be a Type One vampire, most powerful and nearly immortal, with authority over Type Two and Type Three vampires.

41. Welch, *Feminist Ethic of Risk*, 178.

difficult, and oftentimes fruitless with any number of failures and setbacks, requiring what he terms a "theology of hope":

> [H]ope fulfills a mobilizing and liberating function in history. Its function is not very obvious, but it is real and deep . . . [T]his will be true only if hope in the future seeks roots in the present, if it takes shape in daily events with their joys to experience but also with their injustices to eliminate and their enslavement from which to be liberated.[42]

This hope in the future rooted in the present is evidenced in the last pages of *'Salem's Lot* as Ben and Mark, having returned to Jerusalem's Lot after hiding out in Mexico, are determined to end the vampiric oppression which has fully engulfed the town. Ben says, "Maybe it could be finished in 'Salem's Lot by the time the first snow flew. Maybe it would never be finished. No guarantee, one way or the other. But without . . . something . . . to drive them out, to upset them, there would be no chance at all."[43] Ben and Mark, with no promise of a transformative future, are mobilized by hope, mobilized by the gift of their solidarity, mobilized by a supernatural enslavement from which an entire population need liberated. And it is through these stories that a rich literary and cinematic tradition emerges of the struggle for emancipation against unspeakable oppression; individual chronicles that have evolved over the last century into a canon of resistance, historical markers containing accounts of events and relationships that, quite literally, serve as a form of scriptural authority in the hearts and minds of the community that embraces them, discovering the undeniable power and enduring charisma of the traditional vampire narrative within popular culture.

---

42. Gutiérrez, *A Theology of Liberation*, 125.
43. King, *'Salem's Lot*, 404.

EPILOGUE

Staking Claim to the Narrative: The Vampire as Essential Religious Symbol

"I grew up in Mexico, and there Catholicism is more a cultural thing than really a faith thing. But I've always felt that the whole religious cosmology was potentially frightening. Not just the satanic part, the Devil and demons, but their relationship to angels and God . . . I personally am not a religious person, but as a mythology it's very, very powerful . . . that is kind of sinister in its own way."

−*RODRIGO GUDINO, FOUNDER AND PUBLISHER,*
RUE MORGUE MAGAZINE[1]

IN HIS SHORT STORY entitled "Following the Way," author Alan Ryan makes the implicit religious implications of the vampire narrative rather explicit when he spins a yarn revolving around Regis, a young man struggling with whether he should become a Jesuit priest. He encounters Father Day, a Catholic priest from his past, who eventually reveals to Regis that the members of the Jesuit order are, in fact, vampires.

> "You can live forever," he said.
> I looked at him.
> He said it again, more slowly. "You can live forever."
> It was my turn. "How?" I said.

---

1. Berman, "*Rue Morgue* Founder in Production on First Feature," 8.

He raised his wine glass toward me. It reflected the light from
a lamp and glowed ruby red.
"This is the cup of my blood," he said. "Take and drink of it."
He was smiling.[2]

In this brief thirty-year-old tale, Ryan encapsulates the concepts and
ideas contained in this book. And while an attempt has been made here to
expose, collect, and analyze the theological underpinnings of the traditional
vampire narrative within popular culture, it must be noted that, with a literary
and cinematic figure that has spawned such an unfathomably vast mythology, it would be impossible to construct a coherent and sensible theological
framework from which to develop any type of legitimate belief structure of
the nature that Regis and Father Day ultimately bow in reverence to.

While some researchers such as Susannah Clements view the traditional narratives as direct allegories and lessons in Christian faith, it has
been demonstrated that such a position is perilous at best. Forcing the
vampire narrative into any type of systematic theology is somewhat of a
pointless exercise versus approaching the mythos and its subtext as a theological lens through which to view a myriad of religious dogma and ideologies. The traditional vampire narrative consistently draws on any number
of familiar religious elements, motifs, and structures, making it a relevant
and imaginative interpretive model through which to discuss pertinent
theological topics such as the nature of the Divine, theodicy, the created
order, and sin. Even as society and popular culture has progressed and
changed, the vampire has followed suit. While some of the more overt religious themes within the traditional mythos have fallen away, the figure still
exists as a powerful representation of topics ranging from an understanding of death, the importance of sacrifice, the need for redemption, and the
struggle for freedom against resolutely oppressive and despotic forces. Paul
Tillich writes, "Religious symbols are distinguished from others by the fact
that they are a representation of that which is unconditionally beyond the
conceptual sphere; they point to the ultimate reality implied in the religious
act, to what concerns us ultimately,"[3] a role the vampire undoubtedly fulfills
as a form of cinematic and literary expression, despite its modern and more
secularized nature as of late.

It is difficult for the vampire to not, in some manner, serve as a religious symbol. And that symbol is far from fixed or unchangeable, existing

2. Ryan, "Following the Way," in *The Penguin Book of Vampire Stories*, 572.
3. Tillich, "The Religious Symbol," 17.

as a flexible history that spills over and beyond the unwavering Christian allegory some demand it to represent. Rather, the vampire is a resourceful and visionary canon, constantly mutating into whatever form a culture or society needs to it be.

One of the functions of the traditional vampire narrative is to invoke a sense of dread and horror at the potential inversion of the accepted sacred order constructed by God. This analytical approach provides several potential points of metaphorical representation, the principal of which is an emphasis on the undead as modeled by this frightening inversion and the establishment of the vampire in a dualistic cosmogonic universe as the antithesis to the Divine, an agent of absolute evil in a Manichean moral framework where the powers of darkness, despite their attempts to pervert the created order, ultimately fail. This failure proves the *rightness* of the sacred, and provides an acceptable storyline whereby the problem of theodicy is given purpose and meaning. Hallab writes:

> [W]e need [the vampire] to confirm the existence of the Good, of the supernatural and transcendent Force or Providence that compels all life toward a worthwhile and rewarding future . . . The Devil helps us to believe in a good God . . . he makes evil easier to define and locate, and thus he makes it easier to comprehend the opposing goodness of God — and of the happy immortality He promises . . . Once we accept the vampire, we accept the whole package. This Adversary from the Dark Side becomes a witness for Christianity, standing in for Satan in the great combat myth that pervades Christian tradition.[4]

On a deeper level, the vampire serves as more than just another vehicle of Christian proselytizing, it also performs as symbolic literature and cinema in order to conceptualize, address, and wrestle with disquieting theological and social theories. The unsettling apparent enmeshment between the sacred and the profane, as well as the horrific history and symbolism of religion that is often hidden in modern religious practices, are given life through the theological talisman of the undead.

The vampire, then, serves a dual purpose, emerging from the undercurrents of the human psyche in order to entertain audiences while also providing the reassurance of ultimate Good conquering absolute Evil (unless, of course, the vampire ultimately returns). And, evident in the novel *Midnight Mass*, the vampire also exists as a lens through which to analyze

4. Hallab, *Vampire God*, 94, 96.

ancient questions about death, the quandary of evil, the role of religious symbols, the search for transcendent meaning, and where exactly God fits into it all. In the novel, Father Joe, lamenting what has become of his world and his church amidst the vampire apocalypse, says, "It's as if the laws of our world have been suspended where the undead are concerned." To this, his friend Rabbi Zev asks, "Suspended by whom? Or what?" Father Joe replies, "*There's* a question I'd like answered."[5] The vampire, if a theological monster, forces us to examine why the Divine allows sin, evil, and the monstrous to exist at all.

Thusly, the vampire narrative within popular culture can be viewed as an advocate for a new theology, one of transcendence over immanence, a theological exercise that places the emphasis of interpretive religious ethics and ideology on the shoulders of the community versus morals and precepts stemming from an authoritarian and unquestioned God, a deity that seems to offer very little with regard to protection from evil. This reversed dynamic of a community influencing the Divine creates a safe and imaginative space to discuss theological and social issues without the threat of the obduracy of religious exceptionalism. Sharon Welch argues that the traditional view of theism is no longer needed and advocates for society to view the Divine as an adverb rather than a noun or even a verb. She writes:

> [A] theology of God the Adverb proposes that love and account-
> ability also produce a type of transcendence. This theology is tran-
> scendent in four ways. First, there is the ability to see clearly the
> complexity of life . . . Second, the human community can celebrate
> the wonder and beauty of life . . . A third aspect of transcendence
> is the transcending of conditions of oppression through loving life,
> self, and others despite social forces that deny the value of all of
> these . . . The fourth form of transcendence is the movement of
> social transformation.[6]

This theology of God the Adverb leads into a new view of the traditional vampire narrative, that of a form of resistance literature; films, novels, television, and other storytelling mediums coalescing into an unapproved and loose collection of scriptures relating an expansive story of liberation from oppression and subjugation. The struggle of the beleaguered Vampire Hunters has evolved into a revolt metaphor with ideological roots in the Exodus narrative and finding contemporary resonance within Occupy

5. Wilson, *Midnight Mass*, 83.
6. Welch, *Feminist Ethic of Risk*, 179.

Wall Street, ultimately mirroring the theology of hope espoused by Gustavo Gutiérrez, a hope in the deliverance of the future anchored in the present day efforts of the oppressed, the marginalized, and their allies as they combat injustice.

Ultimately, the figure of the vampire is able to traverse and interconnect theology and academia within the larger popular culture in a compelling and thought-provoking manner as a result of its rich history, mythology, cosmogonic implications, and the metaphorical potential to lead one into contemplating their role in the created order established in the context of religious tradition. Whether an explicitly sacred figure or not, the vampire, by its very nature, straddles the ineffable chasm between life and death. It speaks to the transcendent in all of us, our fundamental curiosity of what, if anything, exists beyond the mortal coil, giving us a glimpse into the bliss or the horror of the interminable while maintaining a cultural currency that, while often buried, is never dead.

All the Damn Vampires:
The Undead in Popular Culture

"We all know that Superman can fly. We all know that Batman will avenge evil. There's all these things that we know that, maybe they're illogical, but we all mutually agree on them."

—*CHUCK ROZANSKI, PRESIDENT AND CEO OF MILE HIGH COMICS, FROM* COMIC-CON EPISODE IV: A FAN'S HOPE[1]

AT THIS POINT IN the book I would like to switch gears, transition out of the academic rhetoric, and take some time to specifically examine various notable incarnations of the vampire within popular culture. By no means will this be an exhaustive listing of the undead within entertainment history,[2] but merely a sampling of what I consider to be some of the more significant efforts at bringing the vampire narrative to the masses.

"Best of" lists are ubiquitous in art, music, and literature, perhaps as a mechanism to fulfill some embedded need to have our opinion reinforced, or maybe to make us, in some small way, feel a part of something larger than us, a pop culture community of believers. I suspect, however, that we enjoy these countdowns more so out of a desire to challenge the results,

---

1. *Comic-Con Episode IV: A Fan's Hope*, Spurlock, 2011.

2. If you are in search of a truly meticulous resource on all things vampiric, I highly recommend *Encyclopedia of the Vampire: The Living Dead in Myth, Legend, and Popular Culture* edited by S.T. Joshi and available from Greenwood Publishers.

rage at the snubbing of our favorites, and to feel somewhat aesthetically and intellectually superior to the tactlessly unqualified cultural denizens compiling the list that just don't *understand*.[3]

That said, the following list of films, television shows, and novels is representative of only my entertainment sensitivities, tinted considerably by my childhood affections, my adult curiosities, and, in some cases, my subconscious fears. I make no claim as to the rightness or authority of this catalog, as I am only one of countless nerds with a self-professed superior knowledge of all things vampire. In the end I am just like you, nothing more than an adoring student of the traditional vampire narrative within popular culture.

Film:

#20—John Carpenter's Vampires (1998)

Directed by John Carpenter, Written by Don Jakoby

I was torn over my decision to include *John Carpenter's Vampires* on this list, mainly because it's just not very good. The novel that it is based on, *Vampire$* by John Steakley, is easily one of the best vampire novels of the twentieth century, and could have been the blueprint for an epic cinematic tale of horror, revenge, tragedy, and faith. Rather, we are treated to an in-name-only rendering of the novel, and one of horror cinema's greatest missed opportunities.

So why is it on my list? While I could have easily replaced it with another film, *John Carpenter's Vampires* has always held a special place in my heart for what could have been. The budget for the film was allegedly slashed at the last minute from $60 million to $20 million, forcing radical changes to the script and the overall structure of the film. It is possible that more of Steakley's novel was intact before the budget crunch, which unfortunately left us with a distinctive but unimaginative storyline featuring the Black Cross of Berziers, the Roman Catholic Church being responsible for the creation of the first vampire as a result of a convoluted reverse exorcism, and the efforts of James Woods to halt a dark ritual that would enable

---

3. Really, AMC? *Jaws* ranked scarier than *The Exorcist*??

vampires to exist in the daylight. None of which bears any resemblance whatsoever to Steakley's novel.

However, before you write the movie off entirely, there are some important reasons why I placed *John Carpenter's Vampires* on this list. First and foremost, Valek, the master vampire, is played with appropriate menace by Thomas Ian Griffith, and assumes an unabashedly gothic look that, while somewhat out of place in the desert setting of the film, no doubt had Hot Topic aficionados all aflutter. Griffith, who has a marital arts background, is imposing enough of a presence to not only make his wardrobe work, he makes it intimidating. And any portrayal of the vampire in the 1990s as a savage monster, eschewing the increasingly popular romantic strains within the subgenre, is noteworthy and appreciated.

And then of course there is James Woods playing the menacing and hardened anti-hero Jack Crow. While nowhere near the hulking team leader described within the novel, the controlled maniacal aura of Woods is magnetic, his intensity and charisma, despite the overt misogyny of his character, [4] working overtime to carry the film through a lackluster script.

The film also embraces the overt religious tone inherent in the western vampire mythos. As Father Adam (Tim Guinee) explains to Crow, Valek, a former priest, was transformed into a vampire after being declared demon possessed and forced into an ancient version of the Catholic exorcism ritual. The process went horribly wrong and actually inverted the intended purpose of an exorcism, the end result being the death of Valek's body and the survival of his possessed soul. The crucifix that was used during the inverted exorcism, known as the Black Cross of Berziers, would give Valek increased powers, including that of immunity from the effects of sunlight. While director Carpenter doesn't dwell on the issue, the subtext of Valek as a dark Christ represented within his own profane icon of deliverance is abundantly clear.

Finally, *John Carpenter's Vampires* gets an "A" simply for effort. As I alluded to previously, the cultural appetite for vampires, at least within cinema, had been somewhat paltry at the time of its release, with *From Dusk Till Dawn* making a respectable impact a full two and a half years earlier, and *Blade*[5] being released just two months prior. Vampires were far from a hot commodity at this juncture, and the decision to produce the film

4. Misogyny is, unfortunately, inherent in the western telling of the popular vampire narrative.

5. Interestingly, Both *Blade* and *John Carpenter's Vampires* featured actor Tim Guinee in a supporting role.

was far from a guarantee of success. Notwithstanding this, for better or for worse, Carpenter dove into his undead production with a malicious and hardcore representation of the classic vampire, and for that he is the first of what might be several controversial entries on this list.

In the end, despite the butchering of the source material, *John Carpenter's Vampires* had a strong opening weekend, making back half its budget and, ultimately, turning a profit, a possible indicator that the culture at large was ready for an incursion of the undead into the wider demesne of entertainment.

#19—Vamps (2012)

Directed by Amy Heckerling, Written by Amy Heckerling

The film *Vamps* was a blink and you'll miss it low-budget gem from writer/director Amy Heckerling of *Fast Times at Ridgemont High* (1982) and *Clueless* (1995) fame. This delightful film follows Goody and Stacy, played by Alicia Silverstone and Kristen Ritter respectively, two kind and sensitive vampires living in New York City who, while turned into vampires at radically different times in history,[6] nevertheless are the best of friends. They choose to subsist on rat blood rather than victimize human beings, all the while navigating a rapidly changing contemporary and technologically advanced society. Goody laments, "You have to keep learning to use new crap that doesn't actually do anything better than the old crap, which is incompatible with the new crap, all so that you can have blogs and watch fake teenagers and real housewives, and its all happening too fast and . . . I'm just sick and tired of it all!"[7]

The film takes many bittersweet twists and turns as Goody encounters an old lover whose wife is now dying of cancer, and Stacy falls in love with a boy who happens to be the son of vampire hunter Dr. Van Helsing.[8] Ultimately, the two vampires make the decision to assist Van Helsing in killing Ciccerus, played by Sigourney Weaver, the vampire queen who turned both Stacy and Goody. As a result of the death of the queen, the two friends

---

6. Goody is about 160 years old, while Stacy was a human when Nirvana was all the rage.

7. *Vamps*, Heckerling, 2012.

8. Van Helsing is played here by Wallace Shawn of *The Princess Bride* fame ("Inconceivable!") to wonderful effect.

would both become human, a problem for Goody who has been too self-conscious to let anyone know just how old she really is.

While *Vamps* is not the first vampire film to feature female protagonists, it finds its way onto this list due to the fact that Heckerling's characters feel uniquely empowered and somewhat subversive in a subgenre whose narratives are often imbued with patriarchal biases, where the female vampire is either malevolent, dependent on outside agency for guidance and protection, or seeking some kind of revenge or justice for their plight. Goody and Stacy are neither superheroes nor wallflowers, they are simply independent women who want to live their lives on their own terms free from the mechanisms of oppression (whether inflicted by or upon them) that are generally integrated into the vampire mythos.

Despite suffering from some fairly lousy visual effects, *Vamps* excels due to Heckerling's charming and funny script, as well as the presence of a wonderful supporting cast that includes Wallace Shawn, Larry Wilmore, Malcolm McDowell, Marilu Henner, and Richard Lewis. While not horrific, the film is an entertaining and humorous essay on friendship, love lost, aging gracefully, and how best to drink blood from a rodent.

#18—Stake Land (2010)

Directed by Jim Mickle, Written by Nick Damici and Jim Mickle

Let's address the bloody elephant in the room: *Stake Land* is basically a zombie apocalypse film. While the pandemic that brings the world to its knees is described as an outbreak of vampirism, the vampires themselves are mindless and vicious,[9] more akin to victims of Danny Boyle's rage virus than anything else. Of course, the filmmakers call them vampires and the movie is called *STAKE Land*, so, hey, they're vampires.

Snark aside, *Stake Land* is a boundlessly enthralling film, one that received criminally minimal attention during its initial release. Centered on the relationship between Martin (Connor Paolo), a boy who loses his family to a vampire attack, and a mysterious man who simply goes by the title Mister (co-writer Nick Damici), the journey they embark on together across America's heartland in search of a rumored safe zone feels more in common with Sean Penn's *Into the Wild* filtered through the lens of Cormac McCarthy's *The Road*.

9. Save for a disturbing vampiric anomaly revealed at the end of the film.

Of particular note in *Stake Land* is the performance of Kelly McGillis as Sister Anna, a (former?) nun who is rescued from being a scrumptious vampire snack by Martin and Mister. Her journey is the catalyst for what emerges as one of the films overriding messages: religious fundamentalism serving as a threat far more treacherous than feral vampires could ever hope to be.

In the post-apocalyptic world of *Stake Land*, large swaths of the country have fallen under the jurisdiction of the Brotherhood, murderous religious zealots who use vampires to cleanse the land of anyone who refuses to acquiesce to their dogmata. Our heroes, of course, face off with both the inhuman monsters as well as the mortal religious ones, heartbreaking casualties and deaths resulting from the bloodthirsty malevolence of each faction.

The conclusion of the film leaves several unnerving questions as to the nature of the evolution of the vampire scourge, as well as planting seeds of hope for the future. Director Jim Mickle handles this balance with a deft hand, shepherding a powerful story that is as human as it is horrific. While *Stake Land* might appear to fall into the liberation motif embedded within the vampire narrative, the protagonists here are less focused on a fight for deliverance from malevolent forces and more so on simple survival.

Of course, the act of enduring oppression can lead to liberation. Martin and Mister convey a grim confidence, a praxis of suffering that compels them through the agonizing horrors of an American wasteland into a New Eden represented in the crossover into safe Canadian territory where the dream of a liberative future has a chance to germinate and blossom into hope.

#17—Vamp (1986)

Directed by Richard Wenk, Written by Richard Wenk

While I was familiar with the film *Vamp* when it was first released in 1986 from the coverage it received in *Fangoria* magazine, I was unfortunately unable to watch it in the theater. In ye olde days of the 1980s, there were no video-on-demand services and the infancy of Amazon was at least a decade away. These were dark times indeed, especially for a rural teenager from central Ohio surrounded by farmland and Amish enclaves, the closest mall a solid one-hour drive away. Imagine, then, my excitement when, after perusing the limited VHS selections of my hometown general store one Friday afternoon, I stumbled across the familiar box art for *Vamp*.

Vamp is a horror film by way of John Hughes, focusing on Keith (Chris Makepeace) and AJ (Robert Rusler), two fraternity pledges who are dispatched to an unspecified city in order to negotiate a stripper for an upcoming college party, a move they hope will impress their potential future frat brothers. Unbeknownst to the duo, the strip club they have chosen is comprised almost entirely of vampires. Hijinks ensue, vampires die, some laughs are shared, and through it all we are treated to some of the more overly stylized lighting in horror history. Notwithstanding the unfortunate *Miami Vice* inspired aesthetic choices, *Vamp*, although uneven at times, delivers as a horror/comedy hybrid and was still an entertaining romp upon revisiting it on Netflix.

Most memorable about *Vamp* is the inspired casting of Grace Jones as Katrina, featured stripper of the After Dark Club and, of course, queen of the vampires. A frightening presence even by today's horror movie standards, her alien allure and lack of dialogue coalesce to create a uniquely disturbing performance, setting Jones apart in the pantheon of vampire figures in popular culture. She also serves as a precursor to Santanico Pandemonium and thusly fits into the role of a Lilith figure within the vampire mythos, potentially viewed as either a source of female empowerment or one of cunning serpentine oppression.

In addition, *Vamp* features 1980s horror genre staple Billy Drago who is typically atypical as an albino gangster, Long Duk Dong is along for the ride, the kid from *Meatballs* grew into a clone of a young Mel Gibson, and Michelle Pfeiffer's sister helps to save the day. Writer and director Richard Wenk keeps tongue firmly in cheek throughout the proceedings, allowing the story to settle into its absurdity while providing moments for each character, large and small, to shine in their own way.

Perhaps another controversial choice, *Vamp* is notable and important as its modest financial success and horror/comedy model in 1986 arguably paved the way for the movies *The Lost Boys* and *The Monster Squad* the following year,[10] both of which also featured young people combatting vampires with equal parts humor and gravitas. Whether this is the case or not, *Vamp* is unique enough to stand out on my list as one of the more interesting, fresh, and creative takes on the vampire narrative.

10. *Vamp*, a decade later, was a direct influence on *Tales From the Crypt: Bordello of Blood* (some might argue that it was ripped off).

#16—Blade (1998)

Directed by Stephen Norrington, Written by David S. Goyer

Blade was *Matrix*-cool a full year before *The Matrix* (1999). This is not to say that *Blade* begat *The Matrix*. However, the aesthetic feel, the look of Blade himself, the highly stylized and hyper-real martial arts battles, and the action set pieces[11] all represent a movie on the cusp of a cinematic revolution.[12] *Blade* initiated a new wave of superhero films, demonstrating to Hollywood that there existed a market for a serious take on these timeless tales as long as the material and audience were afforded the proper respect.

In the end, though, *Blade* is a vampire movie, and Blade the anti-hero, played with intense dedication by Wesley Snipes, is one himself. Well, half of one. A vampire attacked Blade's mother while he was still in the womb, and she apparently dies during childbirth. As a result, Blade is born a half-breed of sorts, a vampire that can walk by day,[13] blessed with all of the strengths of his kind, but none of their weaknesses. Similar to Father Joe in the novel *Midnight Mass* and Angelus from the television show *Angel*, Blade uses his position and privilege living within the dominant vampire culture to serve as an activist and advocate for humanity,[14] seeking to overturn the hierarchical oppression the vampire embodies.

Speaking of oppression, the plot of the film is centered on a plan by the maniacal vampire Deacon Frost to resurrect the blood god La Magra and enslave the human race as a food source. Through it all, we are witness to the efforts of Blade toward not succumbing to his vampire urges, meet his pseudo-father figure Abraham Whistler,[15] and watch him kick a whole lot of vampire ass in adrenaline filled fight scenes that still excite sixteen years later.

---

11. Early in each film, both Blade and Trinity take very similar leaps from one rooftop to another.

12. From all appearances, *Blade* was itself heavily influenced by the Alex Proyas film *The Crow* (1994).

13. Blade's legend amongst the vampire community earned him the not terribly original moniker of Daywalker.

14. Although Blade's motivations have more to do with revenge versus empathy for humanity.

15. SPOILER: Whistler, played with gritty delight by Kris Kristofferson, was so popular that, despite his death, was resurrected for the sequel.

All told, *Blade* raked in over $130 million dollars against a budget that was under a third of that total, ensuring its place as one of the most successful vampire movies of all time.

#15—From Dusk Till Dawn (1996)

Directed by Robert Rodriguez, Written by Quentin Tarantino

One of the joys of the film *From Dusk Till Dawn* is watching it with someone who knows absolutely nothing about the premise, which, nearly twenty years after the initial release of the film, is a rather difficult proposition. Initially a movie in the vein of *Bonnie and Clyde* or *Thelma and Louise*, brothers Seth and Richie Gecko[16] are on the run from the law, forcing them to commandeer an RV and its attendant family in order to sneak across the border into Mexico. On the surface it seems like a setup for an interesting Tex-Mex flavored crime thriller. However, as I'm sure you're aware by now, there is more to this picture.

The Gecko brothers have an arrangement to meet a contact that will assist them in hiding out in Mexico. The rendezvous point is the Titty Twister, a hole-in-the-wall strip joint that features, as so eloquently stated by one of Cheech Marin's three characters he plays in the film, a wide variety of one particular item.

All hell breaks loose, of course, as the Geckos, the family they kidnapped, and the rest of the patrons of the Titty Twister, find themselves in a life-and-death struggle against the rather nude forces of the undead, led by Salma Hayek's Santanico Pandemonium[17] who embraces the role of Lilith,[18] using her legions of demon offspring to devastate the anonymous and voyeuristic patriarchy that is inherent in any strip club setting.

From Dusk Till Dawn is highlighted by the kinetic direction of Robert Rodriguez who has an uncanny knack for infusing even the most mundane of scenes with an undeniably robust energy. In addition, the abundant practical effects work provided by KNB EFX Group is absolutely berserk for such a widely distributed horror film in the mid-nineties, not to mention

16. The former played with typical charm by George Clooney, the latter played with . . . well, Quentin Tarantino tries.

17. Santanico Pandemonium is an unsubtle homage to the film *Satánico Pandemonium*, a Mexican nunsploitation movie (yeah, they have those) from 1975.

18. The etymology of Santanico Pandemonium's name is less than subtle, reflecting her satanic roots as a chaos monster.

terribly refreshing to witness, a stark reminder of the uniform and artificial world of computer generated effects Hollywood films have descended into. All of which combine to make *From Dusk Till Dawn* one of the more unique, violent, and entertaining vampire movies of the modern era.

#14—Bram Stoker's Dracula (1992)

Directed by Francis Ford Coppola, Written by James V. Hart

Despite the title of this film implying some kind of faithful adaptation of Bram Stoker's 1897 novel *Dracula*, it is radically different in many ways. Primarily, Francis Ford Coppola and writer James V. Hart have taken the unabashed monstrosity of Count Dracula and turned him into a tragically romantic figure, one who has conquered death due in large part to his love for his wife, Elisabeta, who committed suicide and is refused heaven. Dracula, upon seeing a picture of Mina Murray when Jonathan Harker visits his castle on business, assumes her to be the reincarnated love of his life[19] and ventures to England in order to reignite his long lost love affair.

It is here where the movie loses most of the patriarchal subtext of Bram Stoker's original novel, as Mina falls in love with Dracula, even willingly taking part in the unholy communion offered by the Count, drinking his blood despite his protests that she will be condemned. She is also quite active in negating the efforts of the Vampire Hunters by attacking Van Helsing as they seek to destroy Dracula, controlling the weather to inhibit the Count's pursuers, and pointing a gun at her husband to prevent him from finishing off her lover. Here, Mina has agency and is openly sexual and seemingly more than willing to cuckold her soggy husband Jonathan until she is returned at the end of the film to her Victorian role as a subservient female.

There are many other differences between Coppola's movie and the original novel, some subtle, some overt, but ultimately these variances are incidental to the fact that this is a solid film with a particularly memorable

---

19. The reincarnated love motif is not an entirely new convention within the vampire mythos, as we've seen it play out in the vampiric figure of Barnabas Collins in the 1970 film *House of Dark Shadows* (based on the soap opera *Dark Shadows*) and the 1973 television movie version of *Bram Stoker's Dracula* starring Jack Palance as the titular character, both of which being the progeny of director and producer Dan Curtis. In addition, the original *Fright Night* hints at this motif when it is revealed that Amy is identical to a woman from Jerry's past, leaving us to assume his motivations toward her are romantic and not insidious.

performance from Gary Oldman as Dracula and an over-the-top rendering of Dr. Abraham Van Helsing from Anthony Hopkins. Additionally, Coppola's decision to use old school in-camera effects[20] gives the film a unique otherworldly feel that sets it apart visually from similar films of its lineage, and the sweeping score by composer Wojciech Kilar is stellar, equal parts ethereal, scary, and romantic.

In addition, the theological subtext is particularly fascinating, as the film commences with a confrontation between the human Draculea and a priest, also played by Anthony Hopkins, over the unjust damnation of Elisabeta, the insinuation being that Van Helsing is in fact the embodied judgment of God on Dracula, a theological war that has raged for over four-hundred years between the two transcendent knights.[21]

Of course, the question remains as to which of the two might ultimately stand as just and righteous, as Dracula at one time fought valiantly for his Christian God and, at full strength, is scarcely affected by the image of the crucifix, demonstrated in the immolation of Van Helsing's cross when they face off for the first time. Dracula, now a towering bat creature, asks, "Do you think you can destroy me with your idols? I who served the cross?"[22] Furthermore, at the conclusion of the film, Dracula, dying within the very same chapel he began his undead journey, echoes the lamentation of the forsaken Jesus on the cross while Van Helsing claims that he and the other Vampire Hunters are God's madmen.

Amidst the considerable list of vampire films in general or *Dracula* adaptations specifically, *Bram Stoker's Dracula* is set apart on a shrine entirely its own, quite literally a living piece of artwork sullied only slightly by the wooden presence of Keanu Reeves as Jonathan Harker. Beyond that, Francis Ford Coppola succeeded in forever cementing the literary figure of Dracula, for better or worse, as the embodiment of eternal love.

20. The collector's edition Blu-Ray and DVD of *Bram Stoker's Dracula* features several fascinating documentaries, including *In-Camera: The Naïve Visual Effects of Dracula* and *The Costumes are the Sets: The Design of Eiko Ishioka*, both of which are worth the price of the discs.

21. Van Helsing displays hints of supernatural abilities when he uses teleportation to convince Seward, Holmwood, and Morris of the threat they are up against, and also when he draws a magic circle to protect himself and Mina from Dracula's brides.

22. Coppola, 1992.

#13—Buffy the Vampire Slayer (1992)

Directed by Fran Rubel Kuzui, Written by Joss Whedon

The same year that saw the release of *Bram Stoker's Dracula* also interestingly witnessed another touchstone within the vampire subgenre in the form of *Buffy the Vampire Slayer*. The quality and attributes of the actual film itself are less important than the legacy it birthed in the form of the television series by the same name. Writer Joss Whedon,[23] frustrated at how his vision within his original script was dismantled during the production of the film, was later allowed to resurrect that dream in the form of the wildly successful and influential *Buffy the Vampire Slayer* television series that ran from 1997 to 2003.

The film itself, while often maligned, is an enjoyable, if uneven, adventure. Director Fran Rubel Kuzui chose to exorcise most of the darker elements from Whedon's original script,[24] leaving, for the most part, the comedic elements devoid of the effective darker counter-balance the television series became famous for. Nevertheless, Whedon's genius for clever and snappy dialogue is evident from the outset, which helps to elevate *Buffy the Vampire Slayer* above the mere schlock the title might imply.

Buffy (Kristy Swanson) represents a blatant reversal of the patriarchy inherent within the traditional vampire narrative, taking the trope of feminine innocence threatened by the seductive and invasive potency of the vampire, and capsizing it. In addition, there is some element of rebellion against religious exceptionalism within the film as Buffy, wielding a cross that bursts into flames as she confronts master vampire Lothos (Rutger Hauer), pulls out a can of hairspray and uses it as a flamethrower against the beast, melting his face. The message is clear: it is Buffy who will conquer evil versus being victimized by it, and the Divine will play no role other than as a punch line. She is, for all intents and purposes, a transgressive feminist warrior intent on maintaining her independence amidst the churning male-dominated vampire narrative desperate to marginalize and erase her agency.

---

23. Joss Whedon went on to direct *The Avengers* (2012), the third highest grossing film of all time

24. For example, at the climax of the script, Buffy burns down the school in order to kill the vampires trapped inside, which ends up serving as important background information about Buffy in the series.

Had the television series never come to pass, I'm not entirely sure the film would have even registered on the radar of most horror fans, nor can I say for sure if it would have made this list. Regardless, the *Buffy the Vampire Slayer* mythos would not have grown in substantial cultural significance without the original film and is, in fact, an important chapter in the story and development of the history of the vampire narrative within popular culture.

#12—Dracula 2000 (2000)

Directed by Patrick Lussier, Written by Joel Soisson

With an average Rotten Tomatoes rating of 17%, it should not be difficult to grasp that both critics and filmgoers alike ravaged *Dracula 2000*,[25] a fact that absolutely confounds me. Aside from some abysmal *Matrix*-inspired wirework during the closing fight scene, the film is a rather superb and inventive take on the Dracula mythos and a criminally underrated narrative that attempts to bring order and explanation to why the traditional applied machineries of deliverance have an adverse effect on vampires. Within the film, it is revealed that Dracula is only a *nom de plume*, and he is eventually unveiled as Judas Iscariot, the infamous and debatable traitor of Jesus of Nazareth, cursed to an eternal existence of living death for his actions and eternally banned from the presence of anything sacred or holy.

The film features a solid cast including Gerard Butler, Christopher Plummer, and Nathan Fillion, who all lend solid performances to a film that could have easily devolved into camp and daftness, and Patrick Lussier brings a surprisingly steady hand to his sophomore directorial effort. *Dracula 2000* focuses on Plummer's character Matthew Van Helsing who, it turns out, is actually Abraham Van Helsing, the man who originally faced off with Count Dracula in the late nineteenth century. He has been keeping himself alive into the late twentieth century with injections of vampire blood, derived from the desiccated body of Dracula that Van Helsing has kept locked away in a vault.

Dracula inevitably escapes and embarks on a search for Mary, the daughter of Van Helsing, who lives in contemporary New Orleans and, as a result of her exposure to Dracula's blood passed to her in the womb, has a type of telepathic link to the Count. His desire is to turn Mary into a

25. Released on December 22, 2000, the film just barely missed being named the far less cooler *Dracula 2001*.

vampire as a means of psychological torment and revenge against his adversary Van Helsing, who imprisoned the vampire for over a hundred years. The apple doesn't fall far from the tree, however, and Dracula is unprepared for Mary's own resourcefulness and cunning.

Similar to the idea of the theological blurred lines that take root in Coppola's *Dracula* where heroes of the sacred and the profane are not clearly delineated, in *Dracula 2000* we are left with the impression that Judas was not quite deserving of his fate, as his actions were a necessary requirement for the fulfillment of God's plan of atonement through the death and resurrection of Jesus of Nazareth. Early within the film, Simon translates an inscription on a crossbow used to slay vampires a century earlier. It reads, "All fear he who walks beneath the halo of eternal night,"[26] a subtle initial hint that Dracula/Judas might be a little more than a monster and a little less than a saint, a lost soul seeking forgiveness from the obstinate Divine, literally left dangling at the end of the film, devoid of his own redemption, yet providing his own form of forgiveness when he absolves Mary of her vampirism before he perishes in the morning light.

Despite its reception, *Dracula 2000* is a slick, enjoyable, and entertaining addition to the cinematic vampire pantheon, taking the intrepid step of attempting to say something fresh about the character of Dracula, ultimately revealing itself as an unexpected narrative of redemption and forgiveness.

#11—Nosferatu (1922)

Directed by F.W. Murnau, Written by Henrik Galeen

Nosferatu simply should not exist. Released twenty-five years after the appearance of the novel *Dracula*, the film is actually an unauthorized adaption of Bram Stoker's opus. The outlaw movie prompted a lawsuit from Stoker's widow whereby all prints of the film were ordered destroyed. However, in true vampiric fashion, *Nosferatu* cheated death and achieved immortality as a cinematic classic.

Most notable for the haunting presence of Max Schreck's Count Orlok, *Nosferatu* presents, even over eighty years after the initial release of the movie, a wholly original take on the vampire. Part predatory animal, part plague victim, Schreck is an ambulatory nightmare, his impossibly lanky

26. Lussier, 2000.

frame, all sharp edges and severe angles, casting frightfully elongated shadows across our nightmares, glowering into the camera with a soundless and unsettling menace.

Eschewing any romantic take on the source material, Schreck and director F.W. Murnau, more than any adaptation of Stoker's novel since, effectively bring to life the true essence of Count Dracula as an unqualified and unapologetic monstrosity, neither to be commiserated nor venerated. Orlok is simply a beast that must be destroyed.

Aside from the problematic issue of copyright infringement, cinematic history would be markedly less interesting if *Nosferatu* had successfully been staked and disappeared. *Empire Magazine* included it on their list of the *100 Best Films in World Cinema*, and, as *Rue Morgue* magazine reports, even the Magisterium finds value in the ominous silence of Count Orlock. "In 1995 the Vatican released a list of films they deemed 'important' to film history. The list was divided into three categories: Religion, Art, and Values. Amongst more obvious titles such as *Citizen Kane* and *Chariots of Fire*, *Nosferatu* and Fritz Lang's *Metropolis* were included under the Art list."[27]

For fans of horror, it has been readily apparent for quite some time that countless horror movies have been influenced by the disturbing and frightening imagery trapped within the celluloid bones of the film *Nosferatu*,[28] and rightfully so, as Murnau's work is still unsettling and disturbing over ninety years later.

#10—30 Days of Night (2007)

Directed by David Slade, Written by Steve Niles, Stuart Beattie, and Brian Nelson

A year before the film adaption of the novel *Twilight*, Ghost House Pictures, the production company founded by filmmaker Sam Raimi and a few of his cohorts, unleashed on the world an altogether fresh take on the vampire tale, one inspired by a startlingly scary series of graphic novels from writer Steve Niles and artist Brian Templesmith. Premised on the occurrence of a

27. Lawrynowicz, "Divinity In Darkness: The Rise of Christian Horror," *Rue Morgue Magazine*, 28.

28. Most notable is the uncanny resemblance between Count Orlok and Kurt Barlow from the 1979 mini-series *'Salem's Lot*. Other notable (and obvious) influences are the pseudo-remake from Werner Herzog entitled *Nosferatu the Vampyre* (1979) and *Shadow of the Vampire* (2000), a delightful film that posited actor Max Schreck was a real vampire.

polar night in certain parts of Alaska, *30 Days of Night* tells the brutal and rather horrific story of a mob of vampires who arrive in snow swept Barrow for the promise of a month of uninterrupted darkness and feeding.

Led by the disturbing and vicious Marlow, the vampires of *30 Days of Night* are about as far as one can move to the opposite end of the spectrum from the romanticism of Lestat de Lioncourt, Edward Cullen, or the many saccharine representations of Count Dracula floating around in cinema and literature. These creatures are a force of nature, unreasonable, hungry, and powerful, their sole desire to consume and move on reflective of the ferocity and decisiveness of a biblical plague.

While the performances are solid (if not spectacular), the cast of extras[29] in *30 Days of Night* exists solely to be victimized. And they serve their role well. However, it is worth noting that Ben Foster is stellar as the Stranger, the human harbinger of doom who prepares the way for Danny Huston's vampire Marlow and his undead family. In addition, New Zealander Megan Franich turns in one of the more intimidating and menacing vampire performances in recent memory as Iris, one of Marlow's animalistic lieutenants.

The true achievement of *30 Days of Night*, both with regard to the film as well as the graphic novels, is that the vampires are actually scary, dangerous, and unpredictable. This is not to say that other films have not presented similar monstrosities. However, Marlow and his brethren are terribly unnerving, and the scenes involving their predations genuinely chilling; one in particular speaks to the theological nature of these vampires as a victim, face-to-face with Marlow, whispers, "Please, God." Marlow looks up and disconcertingly mutters, "God? No God."[30] This scene stands as a stark demarcation of the secularization of the traditional vampire narrative, moving from an overtly religious symbol to one of greater mystery and ferocity, unable to be contained by the traditional sacred icons that once brought the believer so much comfort in their fight against evil.

Director David Slade effectively transferred the nightmare world of Steve Nile's imagination from page to screen, the end result being an unpredictable, exhausting, and blood soaked horror film where the desolate and frigid Alaskan backdrop reflects the silence of God in this post-religion

---

29. The cast includes prolific actor Mark Boone Junior who also appeared in *John Carpenter's Vampires* as a doomed member of Jack Crow's original team.

30. *30 Days of Night*, Slade, 2007.

vampire narrative, and where survival and liberation emerge from the solidarity of the community.

#9—Dracula (1931)

Directed by Tod Browning, Written by
Hamilton Deane and John L. Balderston

I remember precisely when and where I was when I saw the 1931 version of *Dracula* from Universal Studios. My parents owned a grocery store in the small central Ohio village of Creston where, every Saturday, I would cart my comic books and toys to work with them, reading and playing in the basement of the store. I had an old black and white television with rabbit ears that enabled me, fully ensconced in my underground lair, to snatch the UHF signal of WUAB Channel 43 out of Cleveland, the home to *Mad Theater*, a Saturday afternoon movie block hosted by television personality Marty Sullivan, aka Superhost. When I was in first grade the show featured an airing of *Dracula*; immediately following the movie I walked across the street to the local library and signed out everything I could find on vampires.[31]

Needless to say, Bela Lugosi's portrayal of Count Dracula had a profound effect on me, as it has for millions of other fans since its initial release. And for this simple reason *Dracula* is in my top ten, its continuing legacy both in terms of cinematic influence as well as importance to the discussion of theology and the popular western vampire narrative permanently secure, the figure eternally linked with notions of the Divine, the war between Christianity and Satan, and the sanctity and power of holy icons.

There are many differences between Bram Stoker's novel *Dracula* and the 1931 movie of the same name, both in structure and characterization. Primarily, the film introduces the quixotic and more gothic elements to the vampire mythos, as the Count in Stoker's original work was far from the suave and menacing nobleman embodied by Lugosi. Despite these differences, the film version over time has become more closely affiliated with the legend of Dracula than the novel, the two coexisting as parallel universes telling the same narrative.

31. This stack included a children's adaptation of *Dracula* from The Crestwood House Monster Series of books, a staple of library visits in the 1970s and 1980s that included The Blob, Godzilla, the Universal Monsters, and King Kong.

It should be noted that a Spanish version of the movie, *Drácula,* was filmed simultaneously on the same sets as Tod Browning's version. Many, myself included, consider this version to be the superior film. There could be many reasons for the disparity in quality between the two versions, one of them concerning personal problems Browning was experiencing which required his cinematographer to often assume directorial responsibilities. Whatever the reason, it is Lugosi who will be forever linked to the definitive portrayal of Count Dracula, and rightfully so. His charisma and ability to frighten generations of men, women, and children was cemented in the huge financial hit the movie proved to be for Universal Studios, and continues to resonate with audiences today.

#8—Let the Right One In (2008)

Directed by Tomas Alfredson, Written by John Ajvide Lindqvist

Out of all the movies on my list, *Let the Right One In* is easily the most disturbing, a rite of passage narrative with an unorthodox love story between a young sociopath[32] and a murderous vampire at its core. The film is a masterpiece and succeeds on several levels, from the brilliantly understated performances of the two young leads, to the gorgeous cinematography that sharply catches the mundane beauty of the depressed and snow covered outskirts of Stockholm, to the understated and subtle manner with which the unsettling violence is unfurled before the viewer.

In addition, much of the traditional vampire lore from popular culture is retained, including Virginia, a freshly made vampire, bursting into flames at the hospital after being exposed to sunlight, and the profoundly unsettling scene of Eli entering Oskar's apartment uninvited. Even the sight of Eli scaling the outside of the hospital feels reminiscent of Count Dracula scrabbling along his castle wall like a giant bug. And, the less said about Eli's monstrous abilities at the swimming pool the better for those uninitiated to this significant and audacious film.

Most intriguing in *Let the Right One In* is the curious relationship between Oskar and the vampire Eli. While not overt, the film uses their rapport to explore notions of gender conformity, the uncomfortable specter of pedophilia, and to what lengths a troubled child might trek to experience love and belonging. In the end, we are left feeling a sense of discomfort

---

32. The novel deals with young Oskar's burgeoning violent urges more in-depth.

over the events that have transpired between the two protagonists, as well as reacting with equal parts relief at Oskar's escape from his suburban hell and abject horror at the life he will be required to embrace in order to remain with the vampire Eli.

Whether a fan of vampire films or not, *Let the Right One In*[33] is simply a movie that should be seen and absorbed as a work of art in and of itself, altogether entertaining both on a superficial level while viewed strictly as a horror film, or somewhat deeper and more symbolically an essay on the maliciousness and repression that can exist at the heart of adolescence.

#7—Daybreakers (2009)

Directed by the Spierig Brothers, Written by the Spierig Brothers

Ten years ago I read *Vamped*, a fabulously creative and original (although relatively obscure) novel written by David Sosnowski that posited a world where vampires were the dominant culture and human beings were either cattle to be consumed or fugitives on the run. While a different broader storyline,[34] *Daybreakers* nonetheless embraces the core premise of a vampiric planet, one that is facing a crisis of catastrophic proportions as the human blood supply is running dangerously low, the eventual result being the transformation of every last vampire into Subsiders, feral and mindless vampires with seemingly no human qualities left in them.

Edward Dalton, played by Ethan Hawke, is a hematologist working furiously to create a synthetic blood substitute whereby the vampire population can not only survive, they can give up the last reason to kill or harvest any remaining humans. This is somewhat of an obsession for Edward, as he was turned into a vampire against his will and refuses to feed off of humans, preferring to subsist on animal blood. In one haunting scene, he arrives at work and stares forlornly at a large holding facility where humans, barely alive, are gradually exsanguinated by high-tech automated machines.

Daybreakers touches on many interesting issues, not the least of which is the problem of oppression and what happens when the subjugated suddenly

33. Remade in America (of course) under the title *Let Me In* (2010).

34. When watching the opening scene of *Daybreakers*, it is difficult to imagine the Spierig Brothers had not read Sosnowski's *Vamped*, as the suicidal woman trapped in the body of a young girl inarguably echoes the concept of Screamers from the novel; adults trapped in the bodies of children. Of course, *Near Dark* (1987) also dealt with this concept to some extent.

find themselves in charge. Throughout the film there are several clues that weave a brief history of the emergence of the vampire, their rebellion against and war with humans, and ultimately the usage of their newfound vampiric strength and power to turn the tables on their former oppressors rather than pursuing peace with those they had come to see as entirely other.

In addition, the subplot of the Subsiders is an interesting statement on how we treat the impoverished and homeless within our society. In *Daybreakers*, as a group of Subsiders (some still dressed in their business suits and dresses) are chained and forced into the noonday sun to be immolated, members of the citizenry look on, uncomprehending of the reality that the very monsters they fear are, in fact, *themselves*. This speaks to the unnerving trend in the United States of criminalizing the condition of homelessness. Laws, local and state, are often introduced to combat homeless people rather than the actual problem of homelessness itself. These laws are primarily concerned with reducing the visibility of homeless people by relocating them elsewhere or forcing them into our jails and prisons. Ordinances target the homeless in cities and communities all around the nation as individuals are arrested for sleeping or even sitting for too long in a public space. Ultimately, it seems that we are less concerned with the growing issue of homelessness and more concerned with punishing those who find themselves in such dire straits in the first place, an issue that *Daybreakers* illustrates with chilling and sad efficiency.

A fairly low budget production, *Daybreakers* is occasionally marred by some overly ambitious special effects. The script, however, is tightly paced and layered while refusing to take itself too seriously, as evidenced by the somewhat operatic reverse plague set in motion at the end of the film. *Daybreakers* is a movie with an intriguing high-concept premise, a satisfying ending, ample surprises, and plenty of vampires.

#6—Near Dark (1987)

Directed by Kathryn Bigelow, Written by
Kathryn Bigelow and Eric Red

At the risk of coming across as some kind of horror hipster, I am going to go out on a limb here and assume that you have never seen *Near Dark*. Nobody could blame you if you haven't, as the film received criminally sparse publicity and coverage upon its initial run in 1987. And, rather than using the amazing original promotional artwork from the film that featured a crispy Billy Paxton with several small beams of sunlight slicing through his body, the 2009 DVD/Blu-Ray release was inexplicably disfigured with cover art that closely resembled the promotional posters for *Twilight*.

If you have seen *Near Dark* then you know that it is a wholly original, twisted, and violent take on the traditional vampire legend (especially for the neon drenched era of the 1980s), and serves in some respect as the ideological forbearer to Steve Niles' *30 Days of Night* graphic novels. However, rather than being set in the snow barren Alaskan backcountry, *Near Dark* takes place in the equally barren desert of the American west.

Directed by Kathryn Bigelow,[35] *Near Dark* tells the story of Caleb, a young cowboy who is drawn to a strangely aloof girl named Mae. She is a vampire, of course, and bites Caleb on the neck before leaving him as dawn approaches. The vampiric effects are practically instantaneous as the cowboy, walking through a desolate field bathed in the unforgiving glare of a desert sunrise, literally begins to melt. From there, Caleb is unceremoniously snatched up into the RV from Hell and is introduced to one of the more psychotic family dynamics in cinematic history.

While a horror film *per se*, *Near Dark* is first and foremost a character driven family drama that relies entirely on the performances of the lead actors. Bill Paxton in particular shines as the vampire Severen, his over the top maniacal brutality coming to a head in the now somewhat infamous and blood drenched bar scene. In addition, Lance Henriksen's chilling menace is on full display as Jesse Hooker, the patriarch of this American family gone horribly wrong. And child actor Joshua Miller is wholly convincing as Homer, a frustrated older man trapped in the body of a pre-pubescent vampire, his story becoming unbearably tragic as he develops an obsession for Caleb's younger sister Sarah.

Aside from a uniquely 1980s Tangerine Dream synth pop score, *Near Dark* is somewhat of a timeless film, the wardrobe and set design bearing little traces of the overly gaudy decade it emerged from, giving it a resonance and power even by the jaded standards of cynical filmgoers nearly thirty years later. In addition, *Near Dark* was one of the first[36] vampire films that eschewed the religious iconography and theological backbone of the

---

35. In 2010, Bigelow went on to become the first woman to ever win the Best Director Oscar at the Academy Awards for her movie *Hurt Locker*.

36. *Vamp* from 1986 was another.

traditional western narrative that existed in cinema up to this point.[37] One scene in particular is notable of this shift, as Caleb receives a blood transfusion administered by his father in the hope that it will reverse his vampirism, challenging the traditional trope that Susannah Clements writes about:

> It is by Christ's blood that the Christian is saved. And, in Dracula, the unnatural drinking of blood in an inversion of Holy Communion is a means of human damnation. When Lucy suffers physically from the loss of blood, Van Helsing knows that she needs a transfusion of blood to keep her alive. But this doesn't, of course, get to the root of the problem — a spiritual one, not a physical one — so the medical treatment only works temporarily. A religious ceremony is necessary. Spiritual warfare is the only way to save in the face of a spiritual threat.[38]

For Caleb, the problem of his vampirism is proven to be entirely biological, as science, low tech as it might be, succeeds at solving the problem that the Divine is either unable or unwilling to handle. It is difficult to imagine that Bigelow and Red did not have Van Helsing's failed attempt at blood transfusion in mind when writing this scene, and it speaks to the heart of the religious/secular shift that was taking place within the traditional vampire narrative at this time in history. Considering this, *Near Dark* is a noteworthy and important addition to the extensive list of western vampire films that clutter the landscape of popular culture.

#5—The Monster Squad (1987)

Directed by Fred Dekker, Written by Shane Black and Fred Dekker

As I wrote in the preface to this book, *The Monster Squad* was an important staple in my development as a respectable nerd. At a time when being a horror, science fiction, or comic book fan was not as trendy and socially acceptable as it is today, here was a film that reassured an insecure fanboy that there was a tribe where he belonged, one that wouldn't judge or criticize or hate.

If not for this substantial and continuing impact on my life, I seriously doubt that I would have included *The Monster Squad* on this list. While Count Dracula is the Big Bad within the movie, he is more a part of an ensemble comprised of the iconic monsters made famous by Universal

---

37. Even that year's *The Lost Boys* featured the effective use of holy water.
38. Clements, *Vampire Defanged*, 26.

Studios.[39] Together they are looking for a mysterious amulet that would enable Dracula to conquer the world, with little to no discourse on the vampire needing blood or seeking victims to convert (although his brides do make an appearance).

Aside from Dracula being portrayed less as a vampire and more as a mad tyrant hell bent on world domination, actor Duncan Regehr's performance is a genuinely frightening rendering that earned him the controversial title in 2006 of best Dracula of all time by the now defunct *Wizard* magazine.

The heroes of the film, a group of misfit middle school kids who meet in a tree house filled with the accouterment of mid-eighties adolescent horror fans and call themselves the Monster Squad, stumble upon the plans of the Count and formulate a ploy to stop him, assisted by family members, an elderly survivor of the Holocaust, and Frankenstein's Monster.

In all honesty, the plot of *The Monster Squad* is somewhat incidental to the adventurous spirit of the film, a PG-13 *Goonies*-ish adventure where lots of people die, kids curse, and Dracula calls a little girl a bitch. The film embodies the spirit of awkward adolescence in the 1980s and does it with a youthful bravado not seen in movies targeted to kids in the current era. The Wolf Man may have nards, but *The Monster Squad* had heart.

#4—Blade 2 (2002)

Directed by Guillermo del Toro, Written by David S. Goyer

It is not often that a sequel to a great film is found to be superior to the original. Sure, they exist, but it's a very exclusive club. *Terminator 2*, *The Empire Strikes Back*, *The Godfather 2*, and *Breakin' 2: Electric Boogaloo*.[40] For years, sequels were generally inferior products involving a smaller budget, a rushed production schedule, and a hack director. After *Blade* director Stephen Norrington turned down the opportunity to direct the sequel, Mexican director Guillermo del Toro, who up to this point had made one American film, was offered the job. Today, with del Toro's stunning portfolio of creative fantasy films to his directorial credit, this might seem like a relatively easy decision to make. However, in 2001 when *Blade 2* was gearing up, del Toro was entirely

---

39. Due to licensing issues, the design for the Gill-Man had to be tweaked to look less like its original incarnation from the film *The Creature from the Black Lagoon*.

40. Well, maybe not that last one.

unproven. *Cronos* (1993) and *The Devil's Backbone* (2001) were low budget foreign movies, and *Mimic* (1997), the previously mentioned American film, was fraught with production issues and was a financial disappointment despite some decent reviews. In the end, Guillermo del Toro made *Blade 2*, and *Blade 2* made Guillermo del Toro.

In some regard, I don't think del Toro and screenwriter David Goyer were making a sequel at all. Technically, yes, we are dealing with the mechanics and anatomy of a sequel. However, aside from the resurrection of Whistler at the outset of the movie, *Blade 2* can be viewed entirely as a stand-alone film. No, del Toro's objective was far more ambitious than simply making a part two. The now prolific director set out to redefine the vampire for a new generation, to reconstitute their DNA into the frightening and horrible predators we all know them to be, while avoiding the triteness of another derivative sequel. And in that regard he succeeded wildly with the Reaper Strain, a twisted evolutionary leap for the existing vampire hierarchy found in the *Blade* universe. Formidable, hungry, and rapidly multiplying, the Reapers are a danger to humans and vampires alike, forcing a tenuous truce between Blade and the undead world he has sworn to eradicate.

Blade 2 works on two distinct levels, the first being that of a thrilling comic book movie, complete with jaw dropping action set pieces and dazzling acrobatic camera moves. The second is that of a horror tale, the tension and scares ramping up as the Reaper Strain spreads uncontrollably beyond any reasonable containment methods. The ability to balance these two dynamics in one movie is an impressive achievement and one that del Toro handled expertly, enlarging the vampire mythos and setting the bar of the superhero movie to dizzying new heights as filmmaking entered the new millennium.

#3—The Lost Boys (1987)

Directed by Joel Schumacher, Written by Janice Fischer,
James Jeremias, and Jeffrey Boam

1987 was a prolific year for the vampire on the silver screen. *Near Dark*, *The Monster Squad*, the lesser-known *My Best Friend is a Vampire*, and the abysmal *A Return to Salem's Lot* all marked something of an apex for the undead in the 1980s until the 1994 film adaptation of *Interview with the Vampire* brought the sub-genre back into mainstream consciousness. That is not to say there weren't vampire movies being produced during the inter-vening years, however they were not a part of the cultural dialogue in any substantial manner.

A lack of cultural currency was never a problem with *The Lost Boys*. Custom built from the ground floor in order to tap into the burgeoning late-1980s youth market influenced by a steady stream of John Hughes movies, director Joel Schumacher's ode to eternal youth was chock-full of beautiful young people, killer fashions, and a soundtrack that featured INXS and Lou Gramm.

Despite this obvious pandering to the market, *The Lost Boys* is an ex-cellent film and a cultural benchmark, recognizable by both horror fans and general audiences alike. And, in some sense, it is a bridge into the more secular vampire tales to come, as some traditional lore is retained, such as the use of holy water, lack of a reflection cast by vampires, and the importance of sacred space, while the power of the crucifix seems to be disregarded entirely.[41]

The Lost Boys was a huge financial success with a legacy that includes two direct-to-video sequels that were produced over twenty years after the debut of the original film, a comic book series, and, probably most important of all, a new generation of vampire fans that no longer thought of Bela Lu-gosi's Dracula as an undead yardstick. Rather, it was Keifer Sutherland's black trench-coat wearing David, a mullet haired rock and roll representative of the undead, who usurped, at least for a time, the role of eponymous vampire.

#2—Salem's Lot (1979)

Directed by Tobe Hooper, Written by Paul Monash

I have written at length about 'Salem's Lot, both the novel and the television mini-series, so it might be difficult for me to add any further insight here. Needless to say, I consider the mini-series production to be one of the more memorable vampire movies[42] in the sub-genre, if only for the frightening

---

41. It is interesting to note, however, that the production of the film took place in Santa Cruz, CA, which is Spanish for Holy Cross.

42. Some might take issue with me including *Salem's Lot* in a list of vampire movies if only for the fact that it wasn't technically a movie but a television production. It should be noted, however, that an abridged version of the mini-series was given a theatrical release in Europe.

resonance of the vampires themselves and the unremitting ability of several memorable scenes to still frighten audiences.

It is interesting to note how director Tobe Hooper, while structuring a narrative drastically different in many ways from the novel, was able to capture and sustain the gradually building tension and horror of the vampiric invasion of the town of Jerusalem's Lot conveyed within the book. Despite some major character changes[43] and composites, as well as a severe reworking of key plot points and story beats, the ambiance of the mini-series manages to encapsulate the dark spirit of the classic novel.

In contrast to this, the cable channel TNT produced a remake of the mini-series in 2004. Despite a relative faithfulness to the important story elements,[44] the updated version entirely disregarded the various characterizations of the primary figures within the book except, somewhat ironically, the role of vampire antagonist Kurt Barlow. Ben Mears is transformed into an opportunistic reporter versus a sincere and benevolent author struggling with childhood demons; Mark Petrie is now a juvenile delinquent, a fundamental departure from the mild mannered and sensitive student who faces down an undead Danny Glick with a cross from his Aurora monster model set; and Ben Cody is distorted into an ethics challenged doctor who is facing financial blackmail over his sexual indiscretions with a married patient, a far cry from the sympathetic physician who takes a leap of faith at the behest of Matt Burke, his former teacher, patient, and friend.

Most notable within the Hooper directed mini-series is the retention of the complications King established in his novel around the use of the sacred icon of the cross. While Mark Petrie successfully repels Danny Glick from his bedroom window, Father Callahan is conclusively defeated by Barlow, his cross nothing more than a cheap trinket. This ambivalence of the power of the Divine represented through its symbols, while not dwelled upon, is at the heart of the 'Salem's Lot narrative, and forces the viewer to, at least subconsciously, confront what appears to be the impotence of God amidst the struggle against oppression.

There is something uncanny in the ability of the 1979 version of 'Salem's Lot to evoke the spirit of the novel. Hooper, who also directed the classic horror film *The Texas Chainsaw Massacre* (1974), and screenwriter

---

43. These changes included shifting master vampire Barlow from an old world nobleman to more of a wordless beast, reflecting Count Orlok from *Nosferatu*.

44. *Relative* being the operative word here. The bastardizing of the Father Callahan character arc is practically a form of sacrilege.

Paul Monash maintained the integrity of the primary protagonists, and wisely chose to eschew the path of easy jump scares for one of atmosphere, tension, and a palpable dread, reflecting, at least conceptually, the ethos of Stephen King's undead universe.

#1—Fright Night (1985)

Directed by Tom Holland, Written by Tom Holland

In an unofficial audio commentary for the movie *Fright Night*, writer and director Tom Holland revealed that his inspiration for the film was born from his desire to do a modern retelling of *The Boy Who Cried Wolf*. Apropos, then, that soon after viewing the film I was plagued by a recurring dream where I am in the backseat of the family car surrounded by a thick fog as a vampire slowly advances toward us, its face illuminated by the crimson glow of the taillights. The first time I try to warn my parents, the creature dissolves into the fog, reappearing only as the adults go back to their business in the front seat. It is then that I realize, far too late, that the rear windows are down, and the vampire climbs into the car, smiling as I call out again to my distracted parents who annoyingly tell me to stop bothering them.

In *Fright Night*, Charley Brewster is stuck in that backseat, helplessly attempting to warn his mom and friends, pleading with them to see what he sees, the grinning monster crawling through the backseat window. And while the film is infused with a substantial amount of humor, the horror is played straight, and it touches a primal nightmarish nerve, the invasive evil that nobody but one person can identify until it is too late.

Fright Night is a classic vampire film in every sense of the word, touching on the characteristic tropes of the western vampire mythos while successfully updating it for a (at the time) modern generation. The film's unique combination of humor, charm, and hard horror make it, in many ways, a precursor to the tenor of Joss Whedon's television series *Buffy the Vampire Slayer*, a delicate and effective balancing act of tones that could easily careen out of control and crush itself under the weight of its own ambitions.[45]

With *Fright Night*, Holland fashioned a love letter to fans of the traditional vampire narrative within popular culture. As such, he successfully incorporated many of the tropes and themes common in the subgenre for decades previous. The vampire Jerry Dandridge echoes the tortured

---

45. A problem the horrendous 2011 remake of *Fright Night* suffered from.

romantic figure of Barnabas Collins of *Dark Shadows* fame, seeking his re-incarnated love embodied in Amy, who also serves as the damsel in distress caught between the subjugation of the vampire and the repression of the patriarchy that seeks to keep her embedded in her role as dutiful girlfriend.

Also, similar to the female victims portrayed in the vampire movies produced by Hammer Studios, when Amy is bitten by Jerry she is trans-formed into a frightening hypersexual demon, slipping into the mold set forth within the ancient Lilith narrative and the fundamentalist view of Eve as temptress, an assessment reinforced by Terence Fisher whose vampire films and the sexualized female undead therein "are commentaries on the fall of humanity as recorded in the Bible's Book of Genesis."[46]

In addition to all of this, *Fright Night* considers the nature of the ap-plied machineries of deliverance, examining the effectiveness of the Chris-tian cross, the struggle between genuine faith and the symbol of that faith, and the capriciousness and ambivalence of the Divine in the face of evil.

Fright Night is nothing less than a bellwether of the traditional vampire narrative, the vertex of the vampire mythos in popular culture embodying everything the lore had represented previous to its release, as well as every-thing the narrative has lost with regard to its theological underpinnings in the years since. *Fright Night* easily stands as the greatest vampire film of all time, both for its ongoing symbolic resonance and for its continued ability to entertain, horrify, and amuse.

Honorable Mentions:

Cronos (1993)

Directed by Guillermo del Toro, Written by Guillermo del Toro

The film that brought Guillermo del Toro into the consciousness of the popular culture, *Cronos* is a wonderfully imaginative work of sci-fi/fantasy/ horror made on a relatively shoestring budget. Despite such paltry ori-gins, the film won several Ariel Awards[47] including Best Director and Best Screenplay, a considerable achievement for both a horror film and a first time director.

---

46. Leggett, *Terence Fisher*, 17.
47. AKA the Mexican Academy Awards.

Horror of Dracula (1958)

Directed by Terence Fisher, Written by Jimmy Sangster

Hammer Studios made a huge impact on my childhood with their gothic brand of horror films, particularly the movies featuring a fearsome Christopher Lee as Dracula, a role he became associated with over the years arguably as intimately as Bela Lugosi. Director Terence Fisher brings a wonderfully creepy aesthetic to the proceedings, emphasizing the spiritual darkness intrinsic to the mythos surrounding Dracula. And Peter Cushing is an earnest delight as Dr. Abraham Van Helsing, memorable in his impromptu utilization of two candlesticks in the shape of a cross, using the power of the makeshift crucifix to push Dracula into the light of day to face his (final?) judgment. Often omitted from lists of worthy adaptations of Bram Stoker's novel *Dracula*,[48] Lee embodies a Count that is monstrous, terrifying, and a genuine threat to those who would stand against him.

Let Me In (2010)

Directed by Matt Reeves, Written by Matt Reeves and John Ajvide Lindqvist

Let Me In has sometimes been criticized as being nothing more than an Americanized carbon copy of the Swedish film *Let the Right One In*. While an understandable criticism, it is a short sighted one. Similar in tone[49] and somewhat less visually compelling than the original, one particular area of superiority is the performance of the young leads, Kodi Smit-McPhee and Chloë Grace Moretz as Owen and Abby respectively. Both actors bring a gravitas to their roles that elevate *Let Me In* from a cheap remake to moody and disturbing horror film.

---

48. This Hammer production does, in fact, deviate wildly from the source material.

49. I do find it unfortunate that director Matt Reeves chose not to mine some original content from the novel that did not appear in the Swedish film.

Byzantium (2012)

Directed by Neil Jordan, Written by Moira Buffini

Atmospheric with a strong undercurrent of melancholy, *Byzantium* sees director Neil Jordan revisiting the world of the undead nearly twenty years after his adaptation of *Interview with the Vampire*. Stimulating yet somewhat flawed, the film follows the erratic journey of a mother/daughter duo of vampires on the run from the past as well as their own inner demons. Included on this list due to an intriguing and mysterious take on the vampiric conversion ritual, *Byzantium* is ultimately burdened not from the complexity implied by its name, but by the surprising dearth of genuine storytelling.

Cirque de Freak: The Vampire's Assistant (2009)

Directed by Paul Weitz, Written by Paul Weitz and Brian Helgeland

As she was a fan of the series of books it originated from, I begrudgingly sat down with my twelve-year-old daughter to watch *Cirque de Freak: The Vampire's Assistant*, prepared for some derivative *Twilight*-light young adult nonsense. To my great surprise, the film was an entertaining romp with enough darker elements to hold the attention of the casual horror fan, made all the more enjoyable by the against type casting of John C. Reilly as Crepsley the vampire.

Vampires (2010)

Directed by Vincent Lannoo, Written by
Vincent Lannoo and Frédérique Broos

A faux documentary focusing on the fictional vampire community in Belgium, *Vampires* is an uneven yet compelling attempt at providing an original narrative surrounding the vampire legend. At times a social commentary and critique on race and immigration, other times more of a spoof of the vampire mythos,[50] *Vampires* would have benefitted from some sharper editing and focused storytelling. Despite this, the film can be darkly humorous

---

50. Most humorous is a scene involving vampires in night school learning the right way to feed off of a human.

and, early on, unsettling in its depiction of the disregard Georges and his family have for the humans in their midst.

Suck (2009)

Directed by Rob Stefaniuk, Written by Rob Stefaniuk

Suck is a low-budget Canadian film described as a rock-and-roll vampire comedy, which is a fairly apt description. With cameo appearances from Iggy Pop, Alice Cooper, Moby, Alex Lifeson, and Henry Rollins, as well as featuring a character named Eddie Van Helsing played by the seemingly ubiquitous Malcolm McDowell, the film has its tongue planted firmly in cheek and benefits from the energy of a cast that is in on the joke. Part homage to classic rock iconography[51] and culture, part loving vampire parody, *Suck* is an amusing effort that deserved a wider audience than it ultimately received.

Interview with the Vampire: The Vampire Chronicles (1994)

Directed by Neil Jordan, Written by Anne Rice

Aside from the insipid casting of Tom Cruise as the vampire Lestat, Neil Jordan's adaptation of Anne Rice's uber-popular novel *Interview with the Vampire* is a rather remarkable film, a well made big budget vampire opus in the middle of a decade where horror was a punch line in Hollywood. Several scenes dip a toe into the hardcore end of the horror spectrum, Claudia's apparent murder of Lestat and the death of Claudia and Madeleine at the hands of Armand standing out in particular. Aside from the aforementioned casting snafu, and a coda involving the sudden return of Lestat that feels more akin to the shock scares of a Freddy or Jason movie, *Interview with the Vampire* is one of the more unforgettable and historic vampire films of the last two decades.

---

51. Certain shots within the film are recreations of classic album covers.

Shadow of the Vampire (2000)

Directed by E. Elias Merhige, Written by Steven Katz

Ranked by legendary film critic Roger Ebert as one of the ten best movies of the year 2000, *Shadow of the Vampire* is a creative historical reimagining of the making of F.W. Murnau's classic vampire film *Nosferatu*. Positing that Max Schreck, who played Count Orlok in the original 1922 film, was an actual vampire, the film is a dark and subtly humorous exposition on artistic obsession, embodied in John Malkovich's rendering of Murnau, a director willing to sacrifice everything and everyone for his vision.

One particular scene involving a fireside chat between two members of the production team and Schreck stands out. The vampire is lamenting his incalculable age, his loneliness, and his inability to remember how to complete everyday tasks; a haunting moment within a film that is an evocative and wholly original vampire movie.

Subspecies (1991)

Directed by Ted Nicolaou, Written by Charles Band,
Jackson Barr, and David Pabian

Subspecies is a lengthy exercise of style over substance. A four film series[52] that spanned the better part of the 1990s, it was produced by Full Moon Studios, known for their spate of low budget and direct-to-video B-movies, and has developed something of a cult following over the years. It is included on this list primarily due to its ambitious and epic spirit, seeking to create an original vampire canon by reaching back into the folkloric roots of the undead. The dialogue and acting is often wooden, and the pace of the films somewhat plodding, but there is imagination and creativity at work within the series.

Radu, the villainous vampire of the series, is somewhat of a physical throwback to Count Orlock, and his motivations are reflective of this as well. In addition, the overarching story of the series takes some interesting turns and, by the end of the final film, develops some surprisingly intricate interpersonal politics and dynamics.

---

52. A fifth film, *Vampire Journals*, served as a spinoff and eventual crossover with the *Subspecies* series.

The Omega Man (1971)

*Directed by Boris Sagal, Written by John William Corrington
and Joyce Hooper Corrington*

Granted, *The Omega Man* does not feature vampires *per se*. However, the source material, Richard Matheson's novel *I Am Legend*, does, and nocturnal mutants are close enough, right? The movie is remarkable for several reasons, not the least of which is that it features one of the first interracial kisses in cinematic history. In addition, *The Omega Man* is actually the second of three attempts of varying success at adapting Matheson's work. The first being *The Last Man on Earth* (1964) starring Vincent Price, the third being *I Am Legend* (2007) starring Will Smith, a movie that suffered from poor CGI effects and an upbeat ending,[53] neither of which prevented it from being one of the highest grossing films of 2007.

In all honesty, I am including *The Omega Man* here less for any connections to the vampire mythos, and more due to the fact that the film marked the first time I ever witnessed the hero of a movie, Charlton Heston of all people, losing the battle. Science fiction and horror films of the 1970s reflected the pessimism and mistrust the public was awash in following the Vietnam conflict and the political bedlam of Watergate, and *The Omega Man* was at the forefront of that cynical tide. Heston (the very definition of leading man stardom for an entire generation) dying at the hands of the *de facto* villain sent a strong message that America was living in a new world that could no longer invest in the heroes of old.

Dracula Untold (2014)

Directed by Gary Shore, Written by Matt Sazama and Burk Sharpless

At one point in the film *Dracula Untold*, Prince Vlad (Luke Evans), having just taken his final step on his journey toward becoming the legendary figure of Dracula, says, "I've seen Hell, so I know there's a Heaven." His lament, aside from feeling somewhat uninspired, hints at a return within cinema to the religious roots that have grown deep into the vampire narrative within popular culture, a narrative that deals with issues of the soul and the hope for, and perhaps fear of, an afterlife. The film is not great and

53. The DVD release featured an alternate more somber ending that was more in line with the novel.

has been widely panned by critics, but gets a mention here as one of the few contemporary mainstream vampire cinematic efforts that attempts to bring the mythos back to an overt discussion of spiritual issues. The focus of the soul in vampire narratives is the most prescient clue as to the religious nature of the vampire and the mythos surrounding it, and this is abundantly the case within *Dracula Untold*.

As the Turkish Empire demands the unthinkable of the army-less Transylvanian territory, Prince Vlad seeks the power to protect his people and lay waste to the invading militaries of Mehmed (Dominic Cooper), the Sultan of Turkey. This leads Vlad into the mountain cave of a powerful vampire (the former Roman Emperor Caligula played by Charles Dance) who offers him the substantial powers of darkness. The vampire tells him that he smells fear on all who enter his cave, but on Vlad he smells hope and determination. In the face of assured destruction at the hands of his enemies, the future Count Dracula refuses to give in to despair, willing to sacrifice his very soul to liberate his family and people.

The vampire as agent of spiritual and physical liberation is a motif I write about extensively in *Such a Dark Thing*, and Vlad the Impaler, at least within the world of *Dracula Untold*, emerges as a figure of resistance against the organized and corporate oppression that seeks to subjugate and marginalize the masses. In response to such systematic injustice, liberative ethics embeds its ideology within the distress and suppression of peoples and cultures that have been abused and forgotten, with the hope and aim of transforming the very structure of society and reversing the dominant oppressive hierarchy.

Of course the vampire, in order to survive, must ultimately subjugate others, clearly demonstrated at the conclusion of *Dracula Untold* as the titular character creates an army of vengeful vampires to help him defeat the Turks, an army he subsequently destroys to suit his own parental predilections.

Dracula's aforementioned lament of Heaven and Hell makes clear that his tale is undoubtedly a theological one, as he, Job-like, willingly embraces the powers of chaos and darkness, admitting toward the end of the movie that he has transformed from a Christian prince into the son of the Devil, ultimately embodying the troubling theological dilemma of theodicy. For Dracula, his plight as the personification of evil in some manner gives him hope for redemption; if Hell and damnation has become his reality, then Heaven and forgiveness must also endure, serving as a type of inverted apologetic for the existence of the Divine.

It is also notable that the symbol of the crucifix makes a surprising return to a mainstream vampire film by way of *Dracula Untold*, having previously been thought extinct, as the more secular representation of the undead figure has, with few exceptions, devoured any overt religious symbolism within the narratives for the last three decades. However, the grand reintroduction of the cross of Christ into the vampire mythos leaves the audience less with the impression of the authority of Christianity and more the impotency of a faith that seemingly fails in the face of evil, necessitating the use of physical violence over religious belief to achieve victory (blatantly illustrated in Prince Vlad admonishing his people for kneeling in prayer, demanding they stand fight). And yet, the inclusion of the cross is important and noteworthy nonetheless, as the theological undercurrents of the vampire narrative once again are unearthed for popular consumption.

Ultimately, the movie itself is a missed opportunity. Much had been made of trailers for the film evoking less a feeling of the emergence of one of the greatest horror icons in literary and cinematic history and more the start of a new superhero franchise, *à la Man of Steel*. Unfortunately, this proves to be the case, with the dark powers of Dracula being played more as a young Kal-El adjusting to his role as Superman (e.g. learning to fly, extreme sensory enhancement, incredible strength, etc.) than a chaos monster inverting the natural and sacred order. Dracula even has his kryptonite with silver, the final battle of the film taking place against Lex Luthor (aka Mehmed) in a ridiculously prodigious pile of it.

Neither frightening as an exercise in horror nor particularly exciting with regard to its formulaic action sequences, the creators behind *Dracula Untold* might have served the material better by seeking to connect it with the foreboding darkness of the source material, eschewing the trend of super powered heroes and embracing the monster that is the vampire. Instead, we are left with an uneventful, though mildly entertaining, film that feels more akin to *Underworld* (2003) than Bram Stoker's literary masterpiece.

Television:

#5—The Strain (2014)

Created by Guillermo del Toro and Chuck Hogan

The Strain has finally come full circle, its nascent days spent as a pitch for a television series only to be rejected and find new life as a bestselling three book series. And now Guillermo del Toro's vision of the vampire apocalypse is a hit show for the FX network, its first season earning consistent positive reviews and enough of a viewership to garner an order for a second season to begin airing the summer of 2015.

Adhering rather closely to the novel with minor changes and modifications, the first season of *The Strain* is something of a slow burn up until the fourth episode, appropriately titled "It's Not For Everyone," where a conspiracy to initiate a viral outbreak of vampirism in New York City boils over and the disbelieving heroes, so ensconced in their scientific reason, become fully engrossed in the swiftly growing horror.

With minds of the caliber of Guillermo del Toro and co-author of the novels Chuck Hogan shepherding the series, and *Lost* executive producer Carlton Cuse bringing his show running expertise to the table, *The Strain* is something of a game changer in cable television history, a vampire series played straight, without humor or romance.

The Strain, while dealing with its share of first season problems, is one of the better horror series to come along in quite some time. Abetted by several key factors, most notably David Bradley as the delightfully grizzled Abraham Setrakian, a determined vampire hunter with a past connected to the Master, a villainous ancient vampire who looks like a giant sized version of the infamous Bat Boy from the *World Weekly News*.

Despite such a design misstep, *The Strain* also features some truly horrific scenes, such as the morgue attack in the premiere episode, the housekeeper's flight from the house of the vampire Joan Luss (Leslie Hope) with the children in tow, Vasiliy Fet (Kevin Durand) squeezing his massive frame through a claustrophobically tight crawlspace with vampires in pursuit, the unnerving discovery Eph Goodweather (Corey Stoll) makes in the basement of the best friend of his wife, and the flashbacks to the past of Thomas Eichorst (Richard Sammel) and Setrakian in Treblinka, all making for particularly horrific television.

Of note within the world of *The Strain* is the gradual progression of despair that builds within Eph as he seeks to keep his son safe while simultaneously searching for the Master and his missing ex-wife. While the others around him seek to maintain some amount of solidarity within their community in order to combat the oppressive forces around them, Eph has difficulty seeing beyond his own helplessness and ineffectualness, carelessly impelled by the regret and torment he feels over the alcoholism that tore his family apart in the first place. His struggles are exploited by the Master, who tells Eph in the episode "The Third Rail" that he will take everything from the Vampire Hunter; his wife, his child, and his friends, until there is nothing left but despair.

This desolation and anguish is further highlighted in earlier episodes when Ann Marie, the wife of evolving vampire Ansel, foregoes her established faith in the Christian cross and feeds a neighbor to her monstrous husband. Soon after, she hangs herself, clutching the rosary, a clear message that these vampires cannot be defeated through individual democratized acts of resistance, but through an enduring community of solidarity and opposition to the growing forces of subjugation.

Despite the cultural connective tissue of the liberation motif, *The Strain* can often suffer from uneven storytelling and wooden dialogue, problems that increasingly subside as the first season progresses. Of course, many television shows take a little time to find their voice and momentum. *Fringe*, created by J.J. Abrams, struggled during its first season, trying desperately to avoid the *X-Files*-light tag, only to become one of the more innovative sci-fi television shows of all time.

Again, there has been plenty to love during the first season of *The Strain*, and, knowing the cataclysmic events that are unleashed and the malevolent depths the novels descend into, it will be interesting to witness how del Toro, Hogan, and Cuse translate such massive and disturbing imagery to the small screen. Until that question is answered, *The Strain*, despite its shortcomings, has served as one of the more original and epic vampire narratives to come around in quite some time.

#4—From Dusk Till Dawn: The Series (2014)

Created by Robert Rodriguez

When you're an established filmmaker launching your very own television network, it would behoove you to feature one of your more popular properties as the focal point of the promotion. In 2013, Robert Rodriguez unveiled the El Rey network, an entertainment project focused on Latino audiences within the United States. In order to draw attention to the fledgling network, Rodriguez decided to expand the world of *From Dusk Till Dawn*, his ultra-violent and ultra-cool 1996 directorial effort, into a full-fledged television series.

Building off of the basic structure of the feature film, *From Dusk Till Dawn: The Series* eschews some of the more traditional western tropes of the vampire narrative to develop a distinctly fresh Mesoamerican take on the mythos, complete with an ingenious incorporation of the mythical Hero Twins of the *Popol Vuh* Maya text who descend into the underworld in order to avenge their dead father.

Within the series, the character of Santanico Pandemonium, played here by Eiza González, still embodies the elements of the Lilith myth similar to her cinematic counterpart. Her origin is very similar to that of the first Eve, as she abjures and rebels against her subjugated role as the inspiration for religious blood offerings and flees her confinement, only to be pursued and turned into a demon.

However, there is an added layer that effectively removes any potential feminist subtext from her arc, as she is also a prisoner of the Nine Lords of the underworld. Santanico once again finds herself a victim of suppression, forced into the role of queen of the vampires while trapped within the temple that doubles as the Titty Twister bar. In addition, her freedom is entirely dependent on the efforts of the Gecko brothers, turning her into nothing more than a damsel in distress who must rely on the patriarchy to grant her any type of agency.

Despite uneven reviews, *From Dusk Till Dawn: The Series* is violent, gory, funny, addictive, and retains the same razor sharp dialogue of Tarantino's original script while successfully moving beyond the somewhat shallow characterizations of the film to develop a cast of characters that are worth caring about and rooting for. Most fascinating within the series is a subtle religious undercurrent that involves radically dissimilar and competing theological frameworks as the blood gods of Christian myth and Maya lore jockey for attention and prestige through the expressed ideologies of the various characters within the narrative.

#3—True Blood (2008)

Created by Alan Ball

I was sold on *True Blood*, the incredibly popular and highly influential television series that ran on HBO for seven seasons, when I first saw the original and riveting opening title sequence. Set to the mesmeric and now iconic sounds of Jace Everett's song *Bad Things*, we are ushered into the fantastical and hallucinatory world of the phantasmagoric series through a gateway of images that weave a surprisingly complex and effective tale of death and rebirth by way of a mosaic of symbols and metaphors that evoke predatory violence, illicit sex, and old school religion, culminating in a nighttime baptism signifying the elusive redemption that many of the characters within the narrative are searching for.

It becomes readily apparent that the vampires within the world of *True Blood* are a not-so-subtle cultural metaphor for the LGBTQI community here in the United States, despite the contrary being stated by series creator Alan Ball. It is difficult, however, to view the proceedings through any other societal lens when there are regularly scripted lines referring to vampires "coming out" and the inclusion of a powerful religious organization, the Fellowship of the Sun, promoting the culturally prescient "God Hates Fangs" anti-vampire crusade. Whether directly representative of the LGBTQI community or not, *True Blood* is, at least initially, very much about the fight for equality and against oppression, both physical and ideological, that takes place within society *in perpetuum*.

Additionally, as has been discussed with regard to *True Blood* and its blatant utilization of the Lilith mythology, the series has never shied away from the exploration of religious imagery and motifs, embracing the vampire's perceived role as the invasive other in order to address religious persecution. One subplot is especially entertaining, as the villainous pastor of the Fellowship of the Sun, who at one time advocated for the extermination of all vampires, is turned into one himself, now loudly proclaiming that he is loved by God no matter what he is.

In addition, the series explores religious fundamentalism from the opposite end of the spectrum, as the Sanguinista Movement, vampires who believe that following the edicts found within their Vampire Bible is the only one true way to exist, advocate for the formation of a tyrannical vampire theocracy, one set on subjugating the human race and installing them as the food source of the undead.

While the series had its share of struggles over its seven-season run, it is undeniable that *True Blood* left an indelible impact on the culture as a whole, its tentacles reaching out in the form of references on television shows such as *The Office, Saturday Night Live,* and even the perennial childhood staple *Sesame Street.* And while its hardcore blend of televised sex and violence spawned other network genre fare such as the more youth oriented *The Vampire Diaries,* the short lived *Death Valley* on MTV, and the Netflix original series *Hemlock Grove,* none have so successfully tapped into the zeitgeist of the culture as deeply as *True Blood.*

#2—Dark Shadows (1966)

Created by Dan Curtis

A few caveats about the television series/soap opera *Dark Shadows.* While technically not a vampire show *per se,*[54] the series has become synonymous with the vampire anti-hero Barnabas Collins played by Jonathan Frid. And, despite the cancellation of the soap opera in 1971, *Dark Shadows* was a huge part of my cultural development as a child in the mid-1970s, as my mother was a passionate viewer of the episodes that were released in syndication. The interesting thing is that I really have no specific youthful memories of the series as far as significant events or plot points. However, the gothic ambiance and the foreboding atmosphere of the show left an impression on my psyche that still haunts and fascinates me as I revisit episodes to this day.

Dark Shadows was well ahead of its time both in its usage of multiple figures from the horror genre such as zombies, werewolves, and witches, something *True Blood* and the television adaption of *Buffy the Vampire Slayer* would later use to great success. It also toyed with time travel as a storytelling device and created a parallel universe where new stories could be explored nearly three decades before the television series *Fringe* introduced the same concept. In addition, series creator Dan Curtis spun off two films, *House of Dark Shadows* (1970) and *Night of Dark Shadows* (1971), while

54. Barnabas Collins, the ultra popular vampire in the television series, was absent from the show for the entire first year of its run.

the series was still airing, a similar move Chris Carter made at the height of success of his television series *The X-Files* with the feature film *The X-Files: Fight the Future* (1998).

Finally, and perhaps most important, creator Dan Curtis, well before Francis Ford Coppolla's overly romantic spin on the vampire mythos with *Bram Stoker's Dracula*, endowed the character of Barnabas Collins with an undying adoration of his fiancée Josette du Pres who was lost to time 175 years earlier, hoping that his various new amorous interests might assume the spirit and identity of his lost love, a storytelling trope that has become as associated with the traditional vampire narrative as the act of drinking blood.

In 2012, a film adaptation of *Dark Shadows* starring Johnny Depp as Barnabas Collins, written by Seth Grahame Smith, author of *Abraham Lincoln: Vampire Hunter*, and directed by legendary filmmaker Tim Burton, was released with great anticipation on the part of the fans of the series. Unfortunately, while the film undoubtedly captured the gothic atmosphere of the original soap opera, and Burton's signature visually extravagant style played to the material well, the movie ultimately disappointed, unable to find any significant narrative traction as it meandered to an unsatisfying conclusion.

Despite this, the legacy of *Dark Shadows* continues to inspire popular culture through its mythological depth and creative storytelling, viewed in countless contemporary horror efforts that, whether overtly or not, have been influenced by this unparalleled television horror project that spanned five years and over one thousand episodes.

#1—Buffy the Vampire Slayer (1997)

Created by Joss Whedon

An entire book could be dedicated to the universe[55] and legacy of Joss Whedon's *Buffy the Vampire Slayer*. As a matter of fact, the literary entries are legion, ranging from academic examinations of the legendary television show to more popular and accessible excursions into the world of the Slayer. No matter the level of interest, *Buffy the Vampire Slayer* is consistently viewed as a deeply layered and nuanced series that served over its seven-season run as a meditation on such wide ranging issues as forgiveness and redemption, the nature of religion, the tension between free will

---

55. AKA the Buffyverse.

and destiny, and the need for friends and family to walk with us as we battle the assorted demons and monsters we live with every day.

Disappointed with the film adaption of his original script, Whedon was later offered the opportunity to adapt the property into a television series. Seeing a wealth of creative material and potential storylines that could be gleaned from his brainchild, Whedon set out to develop a television series that used the horror genre to explore the equally horrific world of high school and adolescence.

Because of this, *Buffy the Vampire Slayer*, while dealing with vampires, robots, snake gods, ghosts, witches, etc., is grounded in the emotional resonance of characters that, at the end of the day, are simply looking for their place in a world filled with very real, as well as metaphorical, monsters, who battle aloneness in their search for acceptance amongst both peers and enemies, and who desire to belong to a community where they can feel safe amidst the chaos that defines the evolution of a young adult.

The influence of Whedon's vision with regard to *Buffy the Vampire Slayer* within society cannot be overstated. Not only did the series prove that small screen genre fare could be smart, edgy, and provocative, it initiated a feminist revolution within popular culture. Throughout the life of the series, Buffy Summers (Sarah Michelle Gellar) proves that she is neither willing to be controlled by her male Watcher Giles (Anthony Stewart Head) nor by The Watcher's Council, the predominantly white male authority governing both of them. As such, she relies on her abilities as an independent Slayer and the skills and abilities of those she trusts to combat evil and basically save the world from darkness and destruction week in and week out.

Without question, Buffy, throughout her seven-year run on television, rages against the prevailing patriarchal machinery, and continues to stand as a feminist icon both within popular culture and within the academy. In a memorable speech during the series finale, Buffy, preparing to lead her rookie Slayers ("Potentials") into a final battle with the First Evil, reinforces her faith in feminist power and ideology when she asks them, "What if you could have the power now? In every generation, one Slayer is born, because a bunch of men who died thousands of years ago made up the rule. They were powerful men. This woman [referring to Willow] is more powerful than all of them combined. So I say we change the rule. I say my power should be our power . . . Are you ready to be strong?"[56]

56. *Buffy the Vampire Slayer*, "Chosen," 2014.

In *Buffy the Vampire Slayer*, Joss Whedon unleashed on the entertainment world a touchstone of popular culture that not only continues to maintain a rabid and passionate following, its vivid motifs and allegorical style resonate in countless television series today, putting it at the very forefront of the so called new golden age of television that covets, above all else, rich storytelling and characterization on the level of a lush and interminable novel.

Honorable Mention:

Penny Dreadful (2014)

Created by John Logan

I was tempted to include the fantastic *Penny Dreadful* on my list of top five television series revolving around the undead. Unfortunately, it is somewhat disqualified as the show does not altogether focus on its frightening vampires. While featured prominently, the terrifying master vampire and his minions are only a small piece of the dazzling gothic puzzle that is creator John Logan's Victorian era horror masterpiece. However, with the insertion of Mina Murray and Abraham Van Helsing into the storyline, one could argue that *Penny Dreadful* is more deserving of inclusion into the pantheon of vampire television shows than the *Buffy the Vampire Slayer* spinoff series *Angel*, which spent more time embroiled in soap opera melodrama than hard horror.

Driven by powerful performances from a stellar cast that includes former James Bond actor Timothy Dalton, former Bond girl Eva Green, and Josh Hartnett (who has no connection whatsoever to Ian Fleming), *Penny Dreadful* is layered and poetic, with Logan's singular vision and voice bringing a literary robustness to the proceedings, expertly weaving together various gothic tales such as Oscar Wilde's *The Picture of Dorian Gray*, Bram Stoker's *Dracula*, and Mary Shelley's *Frankenstein* into a singular narrative.

Fresh, scary, and creative, the atmospheric cinematography, along with the moody score from Abel Korzeniowski, completes a package of otherworldly delight encased in an unabashed love note to classic gothic horror. The final product is a unique series that is easily one of the more creative and entertaining products to emerge from cable television within the last decade.

Penny Dreadful, while not overtly Christian, definitely exists within a theological framework of the sacred and the profane, with complicated textures and shadows minding the gap. There is undoubtedly a cosmology at play here, although the details are only hinted at, taunting the audience with their implications for the larger narrative and consequences for the disparate characters that gradually form a dysfunctional family unit of sorts. As Sir Malcolm tells Victor Frankenstein in the first episode, "You seem like a free thinker who might imagine a world where science and superstition walk hand in hand,"[57] *Penny Dreadful* dares us to imagine a world, similar to the one described in Judeo-Christian mythology, where gods and monsters intermingle and often fuse with human terrain.

Literature:

#15—Jailbait Zombie (2009)

By Mario Acevedo

Felix Gomez has problems. The least of which is the fact that he's a vampire private investigator tasked by his undead masters to stop a zombie uprising that threatens to expose what the regular world can never be privy to: the existence of the supernatural. From there it only gets worse for Gomez in this noir-ish book series that, while possibly a controversial entry on this list, is nonetheless an exciting and fresh take on the vampire subgenre within literature.

In previous books, having faced down aliens, survived the porn industry, and kicked more than his share of ass (living and undead alike), Felix's fourth adventure forces him to confront the circumstances and guilt from his deeds as an Iraq War veteran that preceded his introduction to the supernatural realm. Seemingly damned to live an eternity with the pain of his actions, Felix encounters a girl who, potentially, offers the opportunity for some type of path to redemption. Standing in his way, however, is a literal blood soaked trail of dead bodies, the mob, and supposed allies that have lost their faith in his ability to get the job done as a type of problem solver for the vampire hierarchy.

---

57. *Penny Dreadful,* "Night Work," 2014.

Author Acevedo succeeds in combining the traditional hard-boiled noir detective narrative with elements of modern horror, namely a synthesis of Humphrey Bogart and *Re-Animator* with pieces of *Shaun of the Dead* swirling around the mix for good measure. The combination is inventive, fun, and capitalizes on the current wave of zombie popularity in film and literature.[58] Acevedo also succeeds in structuring his most satisfying ending to date by paving the way for a truly frightening and powerful villain for Gomez to face off with in the future. All told, *Jailbait Zombie* is an outstanding and superior addition to what has already been a fantastic series of novels.

#14—Bite Me: A Love Story (2010)

By Christopher Moore

In 1995 Christopher Moore introduced us to Jody and Tommy, the protagonists of the delightful novel *Bloodsucking Fiends: A Love Story*. Since then, we have become acquainted with a motley supporting cast of characters, including a homeless Emperor of San Francisco and his loyal canines, a raucous group of convenience store employees christened the Animals, a Hot Topic Goth girl with dreams of living the life of the undead, a nefarious blue skinned Las Vegas stripper, an ancient and sadistic vampire lord, and a pair of detectives who constantly find themselves way in over their well intentioned heads. Therefore, when Moore adds a giant vampire cat into the mix, suffice to say it seems perfectly normal.

Picking up right after the events of *You Suck*, the second novel of the series, Moore leans on the narration of the returning Abby Normal, a love struck vampire wannabe with delusions of dark poetic grandeur, to bring the reader up to speed. And while it is Normal's somewhat annoying, often hilarious commentary that opens and concludes *Bite Me*, the story is still effectively that of Jody and Tommy's passionate, albeit troubled, relationship.

Throughout the trilogy, Moore has effectively mined the pitfalls of falling in love. In *Bite Me*, the author explores the uncertainty and heartache that can result when two people who love each other want different things in life, and the difficult choices they must make as a result.

In all honesty, the plot of the book is thin to nonexistent, which is pretty much par for the course with Moore's vampire series. Chet, the

---

58. The vampire vs. robo-zombie encounter is particularly entertaining.

previously mentioned feline bloodsucker, is running riot throughout San Francisco while building an unstoppable undead cat army, and it falls on everyone involved to stop the encroaching menace. While there is a little more to it than that (a feral Tommy, a crispy Jody, and a rat tail on Abby), the focus of *Bite Me* is more concerned with bringing to a conclusion the intimate journey of our vampire lovers.

Christopher Moore's *Bite Me* and its adjoining series is perverse, touching, and hilarious, often all within a single page, and is a fitting conclusion to an adventurous tale of undead love, hot monkey sex, and frozen turkey bowling. Most importantly, while entirely disconnected from the religious undertones of the traditional western vampire narrative, this trilogy of novels deserves ample recognition as an exhilarating parody of the glut of romantic vampire novels spilling over bookshelves, and reflects, in some respects, Moore's personal journey, an aspect he revealed in an interview I conducted with him while he wrote *Bite Me*: "Tommy's a kid from the Midwest trying to make it in California as a writer, while suffering more than a little culture shock. Short the vampires, that's sort of who I was when I was nineteen. So his personality is like a snapshot of my youth."

#13—Lost Souls (1992)

By Poppy Z. Brite AKA Billy Martin

Lost Souls is the debut novel from Poppy Z. Brite who, during the 1990s, was consistently cited as one of the more interesting voices in horror literature, in addition to being perhaps the strongest female voice within the genre at that time. However, in 2010 Brite initiated the process of gender reassignment, and is now known as Billy Martin, a self-identified gay man who has retired from writing. I state this only as an explanation of my usage of male gender-specific pronouns in the following analysis.

Retirement aside, Martin's twenty-two year old novel still reads as a fresh voice amidst the deluge of romance drenched vampire literature, and, in hindsight, reveals a writer working through gender and sexuality issues through his various marginalized characters. From the hints of same-sex attraction between Martin's story regulars Steve and Ghost, the complicated sexual relationship between vampires Nothing and his androgynous father Zillah, not to mention the overt fear of female biology demonstrated in the act of vampire infants killing their mothers while still in the womb, Martin takes the undead narrative and filters it through, in some manner, the ethics of queer life, ground previously trod in the horror genre by Clive Barker, work designed less to normalize queer culture and more to combat the politics of sexual shame predominant in mainstream society in the early 1990s.

Word of warning, however, for potential readers of Martin's work. There's a reason he is consistently listed as one of the top purveyors of *splatterpunk*[59] in horror literature, and *Lost Souls* pulls no punches when it comes to gruesome imagery. Having said that, try not to let such vivid renderings of violence distract you from one of the edgiest, most intelligent, and tendentious voices in horror history.

#12—Vamped (2004)

By David Sosnowski

Don't let the oddly misplaced young adult romance cover art fool you, David Sosnowski's *Vamped* is a darkly comic, heartfelt, disturbing, at times scary, and imaginative novel that explores the premise of a modern society that happens to be entirely vampiric.

Marty Kowalski, the vampire who, sixty years earlier, came up with the bright idea to flip the societal script and get the vamp trend going, now lives a listless and altogether boring existence. Once special, an anomaly within nature, Marty is now just another undead working stiff, his vampirism giving him no special advantage in life. All too aware of the absurdity of his existence, he survives on sarcasm and irony, a poster of Bela Lugosi hanging on the wall and a box of Count Chocula sitting amidst his collection of breakfast cereals. Fed up, he decides to end it all.

And that is when he meets Isuzu Trooper Cassidy, a human child who has been fleeing the clutches of the vampire population. At first, Marty is excited about the notion of feeding on fresh human blood after decades of stem-cell derived juice boxes, but the child quickly wins him over, and he decides to keep her hidden until she is old enough to be converted to vampirism without becoming a Screamer, angry vampires converted as children who are now trapped in prepubescent shells.

One of the more interesting aspects of *Vamped* is the dark morality at play, the troubling idea that Isuzu, hunted by and having lost her mother

---

59. Splatterpunk is a graphic and gory sub-genre of horror literature that experienced the height of its popularity in the mid-1990s.

to vampires, would be sheltered by a vampire and ultimately become a vampire, willingly and happily. The brilliance of Sosnowski's novel is that the reader becomes complicit in what would normally be considered the horrific effects of long term Stockholm syndrome, the traumatic bonding of Isuzu to Marty as her *de facto* father figure, subconsciously acquiescing to her fate as a means of survival, which evolves into a desire to please her captor and become the very thing that has caused her the most agony in her life. And, shockingly, we want that for her.

#11—Bottomfeeder (2006)

By B.H. (Bob) Fingerman

Similar to Marty Kowalski in *Vamped*, Philip Merman, the protagonist of *Bottomfeeder*, is a typical everyman, somewhat overwhelmed by the tedium and weariness of life. He also just happens to be a vampire. In Bob Fingerman's novel, existence in New York City as a lower-income undead citizen is not all that different from those mortal denizens struggling along a similar path. With a dull and mindless job, a small featureless apartment, a single friend of questionable quality, and a daily menu of blood that Philip leeches off of the assorted human detritus of society, this is a distinctly American vampire, one whose dreams have died on the jagged rocks of empty hope and hollow aspirations.

Philip believes he is the only one of his kind, a lone vampire cursed to live an isolationist reality, until Eddie, another vampire, enters his life and shows him that there is in fact a community of vampires who have created a life of privilege for their kind. As a result, Philip's life begins to swiftly change as he becomes increasingly immersed amongst the wealthy and entitled. Things are not necessarily as they seem, of course, and our sardonic hero realizes that some people were never meant to ascend the social ladder, forever (literally for Philip) destined to keep their heads down and just work at getting by.

While *Bottomfeeder* is in fact just one more vampire novel in the already overcrowded Amazon.com search box, Fingerman conjures a hilariously offensive narrative original enough to elevate the novel beyond standard mainstream fare into a piece of literature that transcends the vampire sub-genre to stand on its own as a superior work of literature.

#10—Abraham Lincoln Vampire Hunter (2010)

By Seth Grahame-Smith

Walk through any bookstore these days and you're bound to see some familiar, albeit slightly modified, classic book titles: *Sense and Sensibility and Sea Monsters. Queen Victoria: Demon Hunter. Little Vampire Women. Jane Slayre,* and *Android Karenina.* Over the past two years, the bestseller lists have been inundated with a veritable gold rush of literature's most iconic and historic characters and stories, all with a horrific twist.

Kicking off this literary mash-up mad dash was Seth Grahame-Smith's 2008 novel *Pride and Prejudice and Zombies,* which transformed Elizabeth Bennet from playful paramour of Mr. Darcy into a zombie killing martial arts expert. The success of Grahame-Smith's remix of Jane Austen has not only spawned the aforementioned onslaught of imitators (including a prequel: *Dawn of the Dreadfuls*), it also nabbed the attention of Hollywood, placing Grahame-Smith in the rarefied air of A-list screenwriters.

Perhaps bookending the halcyon days of this historical reimagining trend, Grahame-Smith returned to the genre with *Abraham Lincoln: Vampire Hunter,* a well-researched and surprisingly sensitive novel that suggests an alternate reason for the American Civil War and the rise of arguably our greatest President in history. Allegedly written by the author after the discovery of Lincoln's secret diary, *Abraham Lincoln: Vampire Hunter* shares how young Abe was thrust into the clutches of destiny after discovering that vampires murdered his mother and several others close to him.

Confronted with far too much tragedy for any one man, fueled by an overpowering thirst for revenge, and driven by one of the sharpest minds in history (not to mention a sharper ax), Lincoln sets off into a world filled with vampires, intent on playing some role in bringing an end to the secret scourge plaguing our young nation.

As would be expected, *Abraham Lincoln: Vampire Hunter* is chock full of historical cameos, not the least of which is the inclusion of Edgar Allen Poe, who explains to Lincoln that the vampires are being pushed out of Europe due to the bloody excesses of the notorious Elizabeth Bathory, only to find anonymity and a steady food supply in America's slavery ravaged south. Unfortunately, Mr. Poe meets his end on the streets of Baltimore under mysterious circumstances soon after encountering Lincoln, denying us the pairing of an occult battling dynamic duo.

Nevertheless, the metaphor of vampirism in relation to slavery is unsurprisingly prescient here, as we are a nation built by subjugating, feeding off of, and growing strong from the blood of an oppressed and enchained people. Despite what seems like just another uninventive and redundant literature entry designed to squeeze a few more dollars from the genre crossover fad, Grahame-Smith handles this historically sensitive issue with surprising taste and grace. In addition, Lincoln's assassination, which could have easily devolved into the realm of tasteless action cliché, is treated with the magnitude and solemnity it deserves.

In the end, Seth Grahame-Smith avoids the clownish and ridiculous to construct a novel that speaks to the heart of our national history and identity, while also serving up plenty of the genre staples that readers are hoping for. Fast-paced and fun with surprising depth to its characters, *Abraham Lincoln: Vampire Hunter* is a must read for horror and history fans alike.

#9—23 Hours (2009)

By David Wellington

The journey of David Wellington from aspirant published author to horror genre literary powerhouse is well documented, and the source of infinite envy for those attempting to duplicate his success. "I couldn't get published to save my life," Wellington explains. "A friend suggested I could put some of my work on his blog. The first day I got seventeen hits. By the time I was finishing up my first serialized novel, it was something like forty thousand hits per update. That was when the publishers came calling."

Since 2006, Wellington has unleashed a consistent barrage of creature features, starting with his three-book zombie epic *Monster Island*, *Monster Nation* and *Monster Planet*, the riveting Laura Caxton centered vampire series that spans five adrenaline filled books beginning with *13 Bullets*, and his one-two punch spin on the werewolf mythos *Frostbite* and *Overwinter*. "I grew up reading genre novels when I was a kid. They were meant for fans of those genres. I was one of those fans. Still am. I love horror because I like old monster movies and all the gothic trappings."

Wellington's greatest success thus far has undoubtedly come through the aforementioned character of Laura Caxton, heroine of the author's vampire tales. Undeniably stalwart and intelligent, Caxton also bears the distinction of being one of the only lesbian protagonists in popular modern horror literature. "She's based on my sister, who is in fact gay. She used to tell me these horror stories of what she went through before she came out. A lot of that went into the character."

Wellington was determined, however, not to make Caxton's sexual orientation a hollow gimmick. "Caxton being gay has very little to do with her character. I didn't even know she was gay until I wrote the scene near the beginning of *13 Bullets* when she comes home from work and climbs into bed. I said, okay, there's somebody in the bed already waiting for her. It turned out to be another woman, which surprised me as much as anybody."

"I've gotten a lot of very nice comments from individuals saying that they appreciate the fact that Caxton is gay," Wellington continues. "But that doesn't define who she is. I fully expected some kind of backlash, but it turns out that the kinds of people who read books are also the kind of people who live in the twenty-first century."

This type of deep and nuanced characterization is one of the hallmarks of Wellington's work. From the adolescent girl soldiers in *Monster Island*, to an incarcerated baby killer in *23 Hours*, to a conflicted lycanthrope in *Frostbite*, the author fills his novels with consistently well-rounded and motivated cast members. "I'm the kind of guy who, if I see somebody on the subway train wearing a bizarre hat, I need to know why he put that hat on. And because you can't just ask people, I end up making up my own story."

"I do a fair amount of outlining beforehand, and a lot of research, but mostly it's about the characters," Wellington explains. "The idea is usually a scene, or even just an image. Typically it will be the climax of the book, the last big scene. Then I work backwards thinking: How did those characters get into such a preposterous mess? When I reach the beginning, the moment when destiny conspired to put them in that scene or image, then I start typing."

In his Caxton series, Wellington has managed to craft what few people have even attempted over the last decade: an exciting and fresh literary vampire series that is neither romantic nor youth market driven. With nary a sparkle in sight, Wellington's vampires are bloodthirsty and brilliant, the new apex predator on the planet. As grotesque in their appearance as they are in their ethics, these nearly invulnerable monsters don't want to so much suck your blood as rip your head off and gulp down what gushes forth.

From *13 Bullets*, the first novel in the series, through *99 Coffins* and *Vampire Zero*, Wellington has thrust his lesbian-cop-heroine Laura Caxton into a ferocious and sadistic milieu of politics, personal sacrifice, justice, and the supernatural. In 23 *Hours*, the penultimate and finest book in the series, Caxton is forced to sacrifice everything, including her freedom, as a consequence of her violent campaign against the vampires.

Buried deep within Pennsylvania's Marcy State Correctional Institution, Caxton not only has to contend with other prisoners who would covet the opportunity to kill a former cop, she must also survive Justina Malvern, the world's oldest and most cunning vampire. Equally enraged and fascinated by her long-term adversary, Malvern overruns the correctional facility, giving Caxton twenty-three hours to either become a vampire or die.

Aside from the action and intensity that Wellington brings to the table, what sets this series apart, particularly in this most recent outing, is the level of realism within which the horror manifests itself. Caxton's incarceration feels genuine, conveyed with a lean prose that paints a grim and gritty veracity. Personally, this is as close to prison (or Wellington's vampires for that matter) that one should want to get without a visitor's badge and some heavily armed guards. However, for the sake of an excellent read, the author's authenticity sets the stage for one of the better vampire novels in quite some time. Wellington has succeeded at carving out a solid genre niche for himself with the Laura Caxton series, while joining a small list of horror writers breathing new life into the vampire mythos.

#8—The Passage (2010)

By Justin Cronin

It is difficult to review *The Passage*, the first in a three-book arc written by Justin Cronin, without reverting to clichéd and overused rhetoric. Epic. Horrific. Touching. A literary roller-coaster ride of mammoth proportions that balances vivid detail with a sweeping pastiche of apocalyptic tropes that are both familiar enough to grasp for bearing, yet original enough to feel fresh and exhilarating.

Written after his daughter requested a story about a girl who saves the world, Cronin's sprawling tale of a planet wide vampire plague is awash in echoes of Stephen King's *The Stand* and Richard Matheson's *I Am Legend*. Of course, those very same echoes are found in a glut of derivative works of dystopian futures flooding the literary market and self-published outlets, most of which lack the extraordinary poetic vision with which Cronin weaves his engrossing and powerful narrative.

The author crafts a multilayered story that, amidst the historically expansive and bombastic set pieces of destruction and eschatological dreadfulness, ultimately focuses on the bonds of family. Most obvious is the surrogate father/daughter dynamic that develops between FBI agent Wolgast and Amy, a young girl who finds herself at the epicenter of the End Times drama in the form of brutal and imperishable vampires that bursts forth from a top secret military base.

Nearly one hundred years after the opening events of the novel, the story shifts to revolve around two brothers, Theo and Peter, the former struggling to live up to the expectations and image of his popular father, the latter trying to wedge himself out from underneath the shadow of his heroic brother. It is their relationship which powers the novel forward, as the journey they embark on forces the two of them to face down unspoken truths, discard assumptions about their role as brothers and leaders, and to ultimately find purpose outside of their somewhat preordained lives.

While Cronin's vampires, also known as virals, possess an origin based in something of a biological conception, there is a strong sense of a supernaturally guided destiny at play within the novel. While not overt, a scene such as Amy at the zoo, which hearkens back to the baboon attack scene in the film *The Omen* (1976), is a reminder that there is more than simple science and the natural order at work here. In addition, Amy serves as a not-so-subtle Christ figure, acquiring apostles, including Peter (the Rock?) and Theo(logy?), who travel halfway across a post-apocalyptic wasteland to confront Zero, the original viral, and his own vampiric apostolic entourage the Twelve, not to mention the assorted visions, telepathic connections, and prophetic Easter eggs scattered throughout the narrative.

While the second book in the series, *The Twelve*, has been released, and the third, *The City of Mirrors*, is slated for publication sometime in 2015, *The Passage* is a fabulous stand-alone novel. While the eventual fate of some characters is left somewhat ambiguous, a satisfying first act resolution makes for a worthy story that can exist as its own literary whole without the crutch of relying on subsequent entries.

#7—The Strain (2009)

By Guillermo del Toro and Chuck Hogan

The novel *'Salem's Lot* was a homage to Bram Stoker's *Dracula*, with just a dash of *Invasion of the Body Snatchers* thrown into the mix. *The Strain* goes a step further, mashing together Stoker and King while adding a healthy heaping of popular CSI procedurals and a considerable amount of eschatological histrionics thrown in for good measure.

Since the mid-1990s, it has been difficult to consistently locate horrific tales of the vampire anywhere in popular entertainment. It seemed the gothic and theological roots of the undead had been gutted, leaving the vampire to become either super powered kung-fu anti-heroes or tortured emo souls who complain *ad nauseam* about the terrible burden of living forever. With the exception of author David Wellington's excellent vamp-centric novels (*13 Bullets, 99 Coffins*, etc.), this shockwave of virtually fangless immortals continues today in *Underworld, Twilight*, and the vampire "chick lit" movement which has spawned the HBO series *True Blood*.

Similar to the undead in the novel *'Salem's Lot*, The vampires of *The Strain* are neither sexy nor brooding. They are monsters, plain and simple, with just enough of their former lives embedded in their quickly evaporating humanity to remember their loved ones and neighbors when they set out into the night, scratching on windows and knocking on doors. They are demons, more akin to del Toro's Reaper vampires from *Blade 2* than anything else, a hive minded geometric growth of writhing darkness that enters New York City on the wings of a fictional Boeing 777 and rapidly tentacles out into the sewers, basements, and subway tunnels of the Big Apple.

The epic scope of the novel covers a lot of ground. The big bad of the story, an ageless vampire by the name of Sardu, is everything an eternal beast should be: powerful, hungry, vicious, intelligent, and unabashedly evil. He does not lament his plight, but revels in his power and bloodlust, always a step ahead of the few humans who know the truth, eager to unleash a literal hell on earth. The only thing standing in his way is a small band of mortals led by an aged Professor, Abraham Setrakian,[60] who faced off against Sardu once before in the living nightmare of Treblinka.[61]

---

60. Setrakian is obviously modeled after Dr. Abraham Van Helsing.

61. In the world of *The Strain*, vampires nest near tragedy, and Sardu's New York lair is no different.

While one assumes that Hogan, winner of the 2005 Hammett Award for *Prince of Thieves*, pulled the heaviest of the plough through the writing process, it is undoubtedly del Toro's fingerprints and imagination smeared over every page. The director of *Pan's Labyrinth* and *Hellboy* reportedly wrote the outline for the literary trilogy as a proposal for a television series for Fox, envisioning a three-season arc akin to *The Wire*. Not finding a buyer, del Toro enlisted Hogan to flesh out the stories into novel form. The success of the book series (as well as del Toro's growing influence within the entertainment industry) brought the process full circle, and the first season of *The Strain* television series began airing in the summer of 2014.

The Strain as a novel succeeds in not only updating and expanding the modern vampire mythos, but also in bringing some genuine horror to *The New York Times* bestseller list. Hogan and del Toro effectively laid the groundwork for what has become one of the better journeys into horror literature in recent memory.

In addition, *The Fall*, del Toro and Hogan's follow-up sequel to *The Strain*, dazzles the reader with a tensely kinetic narrative as the forcible vampiric occupation of modern society continues outward from New York City, with the small resistance movement, led by CDC scientist Eph Goodweather and Setrakian, fighting the good fight.

Making matters worse for the Vampire Hunters is the inexplicable complicity of key officials in the upper tiers of government and strategic power centers, never mind that Eph's ex-wife Kelly is turned into a vampire and stalking their son, and a war is unfolding between Old and New World vampires for control of humanity. Fortunately, Hogan and del Toro have successfully avoided the pitfalls traditionally associated with the dreaded middle act, retaining the same epic scope of the original novel, while focusing even more on the evolution of their protagonists.

In addition, Sardu's plan for world enslavement is single-minded and overwhelming as he expertly moves his various pawns toward the unthinkable checkmate that concludes *The Fall*, delivering a psychologically devastating marathon of suspense, heartache, and terror that is, unfortunately, not sustained in the third and final book of the series, *The Night Eternal*.

#6—Dracula (1897)

By Bram Stoker

While *Dracula*, Bram Stoker's epistolary horror classic, was neither the first[62] nor last vampire tale to be written, it succeeded, thanks in large part to the stage and film adaptation starring Bela Lugosi, in thrusting the vampire into the mainstream consciousness and effectively demarcating a specific contemporary interpretation of the mythological figure for the next one hundred years. Beyond that, as we have discussed already in this book, Stoker used the fictional Count to examine themes of patriarchy, sexuality, and the role of religion to monitor and enforce norms surrounding these issues.

These were, by no means, the only issues at play within Stoker's novel. For example, it is difficult to not read the book as a portent against immigration, Dracula representing a perceived invasive *other* that threatened the very existence of England. When watching news footage of fearful and angry citizens spitting invectives toward busses filled with undocumented women and children, one cannot help but be reminded of the relentless pursuit of the Vampire Hunters out of England into Transylvania where Dracula is subsequently brutalized and stabbed to death.

Of course, most obvious within Bram Stoker's *Dracula* are the religious themes. While the idea of the Christian applied machineries of deliverance serving as weapons against the vampire pre-existed the novel to some extent, the eventual success of Stoker's work effectively canonized the connection between the crucifix, holy water, etc. with the fight against the undead. As a result, the figure of Dracula, and thus the vampire, took on a spiritual dimension within western culture.

The issue becomes, of course, one of perspective. For example, if one believes that Bram Stoker sought to inject his novel with a distinctly Christian worldview, what must one make of the use of violence used by Van Helsing, Harker, et al. in their Crusade-like effort to restore the religious order that Dracula succeeded in disturbing? And what of Dracula's ability to, in fact, stand in opposition to the natural order, to even exist at all? If the presence of the vampire does indeed serve as a representation of sin and temptation, we are seemingly trapped in the frightening realm of theodicy and the conundrum of an angry/loving God who needs humanity to do the dirty work of the Divine. As Van Helsing states in the novel, "Thus

---

62. *Varney the Vampire*, published as a penny dreadful from 1845 to 1847, actually established many of the vampire tropes used by Stoker, minus the sacred icons.

we are ministers of God's own wish: that the world, and men for whom His Son die, will not be given over to monsters, whose very existence would defame Him."[63] Ultimately, salvation from and victory over Dracula (the embodiment of sin) is not an issue of faith, but one of brute force, a disturbing, though not uncommon, perspective on the use of religion throughout history.

Dracula can, of course, be read apart from any scholarly analysis and enjoyed as simply an amazing work of fiction that still captures the imagination over a hundred years after it was first published. However, there is a reason that Count Dracula's image is still the focal point of Halloween decorations and costumes, movies, countless novels, and repeated cameos in all mediums of genre fare. Stoker managed to create a literary figure that was horrifying and somewhat tragic. More importantly, he created a timeless monster that could serve as a metaphorical dispersive prism, easily divided up and adapted to whatever boogeyman a culture needed to embody, a demonic corruption of humanity that was both easily manifested and, ultimately, killed, thusly reassuring a frightened society of the sanctity and power of the existing hierarchy.

#5—I Am Legend (1954)

By Richard Matheson

While not nearly as well known as Bram Stoker's *Dracula*, Richard Matheson's *I Am Legend* has impressively influenced popular culture in its own right. The narrative of the last man on earth standing alone against a world of plague ravaged monsters is echoed in everything from the oeuvre of George Romero,[64] to Justin Cronin's 2010 bestselling novel *The Passage*, to Stephen King's classic end-of-the-world tale *The Stand*, to just about any apocalyptic themed narrative one can cite. In addition, Matheson's brief yet powerful novel has spawned three film adaptions as previously discussed in my analysis of 1971's film *The Omega Man*.

In the story, Robert Neville may very well be the lone survivor of a pandemic that has apparently wiped out humanity, leaving behind a world of vampires that, led by Neville's former best friend Ben Cortman, attack

---

63. Stoker, *Dracula*,173.

64 And has influenced the zombie apocalypse sub-genre as a whole.

Neville's fortified home, taunting him and seeking entrance, desperate to eliminate him once and for all.

I encountered *I Am Legend* for the first time as a freshman in high school. If you read the introduction to this book then you know that I wasn't exactly the model of popularity as a teenager. Matheson's novel resonated with me on several different levels, the least of which, surprisingly, was the science fiction and horror elements. The predicament of Neville represented for me the worst of high school, a sense of aloneness that was further exacerbated by the seemingly endless taunts of others, some of them former friends who had found new interests and athletic pursuits while I chose to continue writing fantastical stories, watching horror movies, and immersing myself within my own imagination. Neville's predicament was a story I could relate to.

Without spoiling things, it is important to point out that, while Bram Stoker's novel *Dracula* paints the titular character as the invasive other that is finally destroyed at the end of the tale, *I Am Legend* concludes with a poignant examination of what it means to *be* the invasive other, and, particularly important in a post-9/11 world, what happens when obsession and hatred blind us to our own works of violence and oppression.

#4—Midnight Mass (2004)

By F. Paul Wilson

F. Paul Wilson's *Midnight Mass* is actually three genres in one. The first half of the novel is horror writing at its finest, leaping out of the shadows on page one and relentlessly chasing the reader through the darkened streets of their imagination until it deftly transitions into a metaphysical musing on what it means to be human. From there, Wilson's storytelling violently downshifts into an action soaked revenge tale couched in the nightmare world of a vampire apocalypse.

Lamenting the absence of truly ghastly vampires in the horror genre, or, as Wilson describes in an author's note preceding *Midnight Mass*, "the soulless, merciless, parasitic creatures we all knew and loved," the author set out to pen a tale that countered "the tortured romantic aesthetes who have been passing lately for vampires."[65] On all counts, Wilson succeeded at constructing a work that has continued to be underappreciated since its

---

65. Wilson, *Midnight Mass*, Author's Note.

initial publication, finding itself seemingly lost in the shadow of his wildly popular *Repairman Jack* series.

In all likelihood having influenced David Sosnowski's equally wonderful novel *Vamped* and the sub-genre busting Spierig Brothers film *Daybreakers*, *Midnight Mass* introduces a world where humankind suddenly finds itself teetering on annihilation at the hands of a swift and violent vampiric worldwide assault. Save for a few regions of the United States the undead have yet to consume, inhabitants of communities around the globe are relegated to camouflaging their existence as best they can, or risk serving as blood cattle for the new dominant species.

Thankfully, Wilson does not attempt to post-modernize his brand of vampire. Rather, he reclaims the popular mythology associated with the monster, as evidenced when he writes, "My premise going in was that all the legends about the undead were true: they feared crosses, were killed by sunlight, were burned by holy water and crucifixes, cast no reflection, etcetera."[66] By embracing this traditional approach, the author swings wide open the theological door that one would have to walk through if, in fact, vampires existed. And by setting the bulk of the first half of the novel in a Catholic church under siege by the undead, and populating the pages with intelligent, determined, and tough-as-nails survivors struggling to maintain their faith amidst the gore and insanity, Wilson is able to explore spiritual questions that have every right to manifest in this type of horror novel.

The pleasure involved in reading a razor sharp novel celebrating the spiritual trappings of the traditional vampire aside, with *Midnight Mass* one can blindly apply any number of positive adjectives and labels; wickedly smart, thrilling, often horrifying, emotionally draining, devastatingly violent, and surprisingly tender. Because of this, F. Paul Wilson's addition to the legions of undead literary entries undoubtedly deserves to sit amidst such classics as Stephen King's *Salem's Lot* and John Steakley's *Vampire$*, two other important literary works that explore the confluence of faith and vampirism by slamming the door on the post-modern revisionism that has plagued the undead sub-genre for decades.

66. Ibid., Author's Note.

#3—Let the Right One In (2004)

By John Ajvide Lindqvist

Let the Right One In is about as dark and grim a novel as you will ever read. Set in a suburb of Stockholm in 1981, author John Ajvide Lindqvist carves out a twisted and forbidding narrative that tightly coils itself around an array of less than cheerful issues such as forced castration, pedophilia, bullying, murder (including the murder of children), and the evolution of a potential young sociopath.

Focused on the burgeoning relationship between preteen Oskar and his new neighbor Eli, a female child who also happens to be a rather old vampire, the novel is a sophisticated love story, albeit not a comfortable one to witness as it evolves into something entirely disturbing, tragic, and, oddly satisfying.

Despite having a Swedish and an American film adaption to its credit, *Let the Right One In* surprisingly still contains a plethora of untapped resources within the novel, such as a frightening subplot involving Eli's caretaker Håkan and his monstrous evolution, the corrupt and sick history of the disgraced teacher made flesh as he mindlessly pursues his previously contained hunger.

Let the Right One In is a dangerous work of horror literature, one with assorted sharp edges that hold the potential to slice open the reader as it eschews conventions and social norms. John Ajvide Lindqvist cuts through the outer layers of acceptability and pulls back the flesh to reveal a world that is, aside from the presence of vampires, all too real, all too horrific; it is the world of adolescence.

#2—Vampire$ (1990)

By John Steakley

John Steakley's novel *Vampire$* is simply a massive and enthralling endeavor, an action-adventure/horror hybrid turned up well past eleven. From the swaggering, tougher-than-nails John Wayne presence of protagonist vampire hunter Jack Crow, to the malevolent, godlike, and nearly indestructible nature of the vampires, to the embodiment of literary tropes enlarged to mammoth proportions, this is a literary experience that leaves the reader tattered, bruised, and beaten.

The premise is a simple yet intriguing one: vampires are real, they are evil, and Vampire$, Inc. kills them, for a hefty fee of course. Around this skeleton a considerable amount of sinew and flesh is developed by Steakley, musing on everything from the corrupting influence of wealth amidst certain pockets of society, to the nature of religion and the role of the Divine when it comes to the existence of evil, particularly the evil embodied specifically in the terrifying manifestation of the vampire.

Steakley excels at balancing the breathless action of the novel with surprisingly layered character development that evolves from hardboiled macho stereotypes and femme fatale caricatures into far more complex profiles of fear, courage, friendship, love, and solidarity. The darkly writhing twists and turns that transpire throughout the story are less shocking for their suddenness or plot consequences, and more so because of their impact and emotional toll the increasingly devastating events take on the characters.

While Steakley's novel received a modest amount of attention during the release of John Carpenter's misguided and severely flawed film adaptation in 1998, this is a book that has been criminally overlooked for over twenty years. An imaginative take on the vampire subgenre, Steakley's *Vampire$* still stands as an inventive and original reformulation of the Vampire Hunter motif, a jet-fueled narrative that does not let up until the surprisingly thoughtful conclusion.

#1—'Salem's Lot (1975)

By Stephen King

Having discussed it at length throughout this book, it should be clear by now that I view *'Salem's Lot* as something more than a simple horror novel about vampires systematically consuming a small backwoods town in Maine. And while it is somewhat difficult to add much more in the way of theological analysis of the novel at this time, it is, without equivocation, the Great American Novel, reflecting a mistrust and paranoia growing within the country in the early half of the decade of the 1970s following the Vietnam conflict and the political chaos of Nixon's Watergate scandal. The book made tangible within the culture a creeping sense of dread that all was not well within society, and that a very real threat existed. That threat, we have come to discover, were our leaders, the various public institutions we came to trust, and, most horrifically, our own neighbors.

Having been raised in small town America, King's rendering of a village that shares in a collective darkness of sin, oppression, and misdeeds, a middle America locale burdened by unspoken wickedness residing just under the surface of its pastoral facade, resonates even louder today. As I write this, the undead cadavers buried in the shallow graves of racism and police brutality have reared their ugly heads in Ferguson, Missouri, with the shocking and violent events surrounding the police shooting of Michael Brown (and the subsequent refusal of a grand jury to indict police officer Darren Wilson), who was seemingly guilty, first and foremost, of being a black American. In the novel 'Salem's Lot, Barlow and Straker, two men of considerable and unabashed evil, take great comfort that their soulless presence and endeavors will be masked in part by the nearly equal soulless condition of a town seeking to bathe their own misdeeds in shadow.

Brief academic analysis aside, 'Salem's Lot also happens to be one of the scariest novels of all time, casting a long and ominous silhouette over all other vampire narratives before and after its publication, a veritable Marsten House of literary power. While set in the 1970s, the chills that King weaves throughout his dark tapestry are timeless and effective, an abiding fairy tale of ultimate evil basking in the pastoral mosaic of an imagined "real" America that has never really existed, and serves as a fitting denouement to *Such a Dark Thing*, standing as a prime example of how the vampire narrative is able to emerge out of society in an absorbing manner as a result of its allegorical and metaphorical potential to dissect the theological and sociological underpinnings of popular culture.

Bibliography

30 Days of Night. DVD. Directed by David Slade. 2007; Los Angeles, CA: Columbia Pictures, 2008. DVD.

Asma, Stephen T. *On Monsters: An Unnatural History of Our Worst Fears*. Oxford: Oxford University Press, 2009.

Baudrillard, Jean. *Simulacra and Simulation*. Ann Arbor: University of Michigan Press, 1994.

Beal, Timothy K. *Religion and Its Monsters*. New York: Routledge, 2002.

Berman, A.S. "*Rue Morgue* Founder in Production on First Feature." *Rue Morgue Magazine*, October 2011.

Bram Stoker's Dracula. DVD. Directed by Francis Ford Coppola. 1992; Los Angeles, CA: Sony Pictures, 2007.

Brueggemann, Walter. *Journey to the Common Good*. Louisville: Westminster John Knox Press, 2010.

Buffy the Vampire Slayer. "Chosen," episode 144, September 14, 2014 (originally aired May 20, 2003).

Buffy the Vampire Slayer. "Never Kill a Boy on the First Date," episode 5, September 14, 2014 (originally aired March 31, 1997).

Byzantium. DVD. Directed by Neil Jordan. 2013; London, England: Studio Canal, 2013.

Cabin in the Woods, The. DVD. Directed by Drew Goddard. 2012; Santa Monica, CA: Lionsgate, 2012.

Christian Science Monitor, The. "Glenn Beck Stick 'Liberation Theology Label on Obama's Christianity." Last modified August 25, 2010. Accessed September 2, 2014. http://www.csmonitor.com/USA/Politics/The-Vote/2010/0825/Glenn-Beck-sticks-liberation-theology-label-on-Obama-s-Christianity.

Clements, Susannah. *The Vampire Defanged: How the Embodiment of Evil Became a Romantic Hero*. Grand Rapids: Brazos Press, 2011.

Comic-Con Episode IV: A Fan's Hope. DVD. Directed by Morgan Spurlock. 2011. New York, NY: E1 Entertainment, 2011.

Cone, James H. "A Black Theology of Liberation." In *Readings in Christian Ethics: A Historical Sourcebook*, edited by J. Philip Wogaman and Douglas M. Strong, 358–362. Louisville: Westminster/John Knox Press, 1996.

Cowan, Douglas E. *Sacred Terror: Religion and Horror on the Silver Screen*. Waco: Baylor University Press, 2008.

Dracula 2000. DVD. Directed by Patrick Lussier. 2000; Los Angeles, CA: Dimension Films, 2001.

Bibliography

Edwards, Jonathan. *A Jonathan Edwards Reader*. Edited by John E. Smith, Harry S. Stout, and Kenneth P. Minkema. New Haven: Yale UP, 1995.

EW. "Joss Whedon: The Definitive EW Interview." Last modified September 24, 2013. Accessed September 1, 2014. http://insidetv.ew.com/2013/09/24/joss-whedon-interview.

Fearless Vampire Killers, The. DVD. Directed by Roman Polanski. 1967; Los Angeles, CA: Warner Brothers, 2004.

Fright Night. DVD. Directed by Tom Holland. 1985; Los Angeles, CA: Columbia Pictures, 1999.

From Dusk Till Dawn. DVD. Directed by Robert Rodriguez. 1996; Los Angeles, CA: Dimension Films, 2000.

From Dusk Till Dawn: The Series. "Mistress," episode 3, August 2, 2014 (originally aired March 24, 2014).

Gaiman, Neil. *Coraline*. New York: Harper Collins, 2002.

González, Justo L., and Zaida Pérez. *An Introduction to Christian Theology*. Nashville: Abingdon Press, 2002.

Gutiérrez, Gustavo. "A Theology of Liberation." In *Readings in Christian Ethics: A Historical Sourcebook*, edited by J. Philip Wogaman and Douglas M. Strong, 341–345. Louisville: Westminster/John Knox Press, 1996.

Gutiérrez, Gustavo. *A Theology of Liberation: History, Politics, and Salvation*. Maryknoll, NY: Orbis Books, 1973.

Hallab, Mary Y. *Vampire God: The Allure of the Undead in Western Culture*. New York: State University of New York Press, 2009.

Hedges, Chris, and Joe Sacco. *Days of Destruction, Days of Revolt*. New York: Nation Books, 2012.

Inbody, Tyron. *The Transforming God: An Interpretation of Suffering and Evil*. Louisville, Ky.: Westminster John Knox Press, 1997.

Ingebretsen, Edward J. *Maps of Heaven, Maps of Hell: Religious Terror as Memory from the Puritans to Stephen King*. Armonk, New York: M.E. Sharpe, 1996.

Isasi-Diaz, Ada Maria. "Love of Neighbor in the 1980s." In *Feminist Theological Ethics*, edited by Lois K. Daly, 77–86. Louisville: Westminster/John Knox Press, 1994.

Johnson, Judith E. "Women and Vampires: Nightmare or Utopia?" *Kenyon Review* 15:1 72–80, 1993.

Joshi, S. T. "Religion and Vampires." In *Encyclopedia of the Vampire the Living Dead in Myth, Legend, and Popular Culture*, edited by S.T. Joshi, 244–53. Westport: Greenwood, 2011.

Kazantzakis, Nikos. *The Last Temptation of Christ*. New York: Simon and Schuster, 1960.

Kearney, Richard. *Strangers, Gods, and Monsters: Interpreting Otherness*. New York: Routledge, 2003.

King, Stephen. *Danse Macabre*. New York: Everest House, 1981.

King, Stephen. *'Salem's Lot*. New York: Doubleday, 1975.

Leeming, David, and Jake Page. *Goddess: Myths of the Female Divine*. Oxford: Oxford University Press, 1994.

Leggett, Paul. *Terence Fisher: Horror, Myth and Religion*. North Carolina: McFarland, 2002.

Lawrynowicz, Lea. "Divinity In Darkness: The Rise of Christian Horror." *Rue Morgue Magazine*, March, 2009.

Lost Boys, The. DVD. Directed by Joel Schumacher. 1987; Los Angeles, CA: Warner Brothers, 1998.

Lovecraft, H. P. *The Call of Cthulhu.* Adelaide: The University of Adelaide Library, 1926.

Matheson, Richard. *I Am Legend.* New York: Eclipse Books, 1954.

McDonald, Beth E. *The Vampire as Numinous Experience: Spiritual Journeys with the Undead in British and American Literature.* Jefferson, N.C.: McFarland & Co., Publishers, 2004.

McGrath, Alister E. *Theology: The Basics.* 2nd ed. Malden, MA: Blackwell Publications, 2008.

Mitchell, Nathan D. *Meeting Mystery.* New York: Orbis Books, 2006.

Otto, Rudolf. *The Idea of the Holy: An Inquiry into the Non-Rational Factor in the Idea of the Divine and its Relation to the Rational.* New York: Oxford University Press, 1958.

Paffenroth, Kim. *Gospel of the Living Dead: George Romero's Visions of Hell on Earth.* Waco: Baylor University Press, 2006.

Penny Dreadful. "Night Work," episode 1, September 22, 2014 (originally aired May 21, 2014).

Poole, W. Scott. *Monsters in America: Our Historical Obsessions with the Hideous and the Haunting.* Waco: Baylor University Press, 2011.

Prophecy, The. DVD. Directed by Gregory Widen. 1995; Los Angeles, CA: Dimension Films, 1999.

Religion Dispatches. "Glenn Beck Takes on Liberation Theology." Last modified July 19, 2010. Accessed September 2, 2014. http://religiondispatches.org/glenn-beck-takes-on-liberation-theology/.

Rice, Anne. *Interview with the Vampire.* New York: Knopf, 1976.

Ryan, Alan. "Following the Way." In *The Penguin Book of Vampire Stories,* edited by Alan Ryan, 562–573. London, England: Penguin Books, 1988.

Sanford, John A. *The Strange Trial of Mr. Hyde: A New Look at the Nature of Human Evil.* San Francisco: Harper & Row, 1987.

Schneider, Kirk J. *Horror and the Holy: Wisdom-Teachings of the Monster Tale.* London: Open Court, 1993.

Steakley, John. *Vampire$.* New York: Roc Book, 1990.

Stoker, Bram. *Dracula.* Charlottesville, VA: University of Virginia Library, 1996.

Tillich, Paul. "The Religious Symbol." In *Myth and Symbol,* edited by F.W. Dillistone, 15–34. Essex: The Talbot Press, 1966.

Vamps. DVD. Directed by Amy Heckerling. Los Angeles, CA: Anchor Bay Films, 2012.

Welch, Sharon D. *A Feminist Ethic of Risk,* Minneapolis: Augsburg Fortress Press, 2000.

Wilde, Oscar. *The Picture of Dorian Grey.* Oxford: Oxford University Press, 2000.

Wilson, F. Paul. *Midnight Mass.* New York: Tor Books, 2004.

Winter, Douglas E. *Stephen King: The Art of Darkness.* New York: New American Library, 1984.

Yarbro, Chelsea Quinn. *Hôtel Transylvania: A Novel of Forbidden Love.* New York: St. Martin's Press, 1978.

Index

Index

Index